HINTS and TIPS
for the
HANDYMAN

HINTS and TIPS
for the
HANDYMAN

by
Bernard Gladstone

PITMAN PUBLISHING CORPORATION
New York   Toronto   London

1.1

Associated Companies
Sir Isaac Pitman & Sons, Ltd.
London   Melbourne   Johannesburg
Sir Isaac Pitman & Sons (Canada), Ltd.
Toronto

Library of Congress Catalog Card Number 60-13427

Printed in The United States of America

INTRODUCTION

This book is intended for everyone who is interested in saving either time or money, or both. The hundreds of time-saving short cuts and money-saving tips included in these pages will prove of value to the homeowner and the apartment dweller alike—and to the lady of the house as well as the man.

Though not primarily intended to serve as a typical "how-to" manual with detailed descriptions of all basic handyman techniques, this book does include many tips which contain important information for the beginner. However, for the most part, the pages which follow will devote themselves almost entirely to describing quicker and easier methods for performing all types of simple home repairs—the kind of repairs which everyone is faced with at one time or another.

Many of the tips tell how to "make-do" in an emergency when the proper tool is not immediately at hand, while others tell how to improvise when a temporary repair must be hurriedly made. As a glance at the table of contents will indicate, practically every part of the house and its contents have been covered. The short cuts described have all been tested over the years, and have proved workable by thousands of craftsmen, both amateur and professional. Many of the tips are of the "Why didn't I think of that before?" category. Others are actually trade secrets with which only experienced craftsmen are normally familiar.

It is for these reasons that it can be safely said that this book will prove of equal value to the experienced handyman as well as to the neophyte. To the handyman it offers a wealth of valuable suggestions on how difficult jobs can be made easier or quicker. To the beginner it can serve as a guide which describes in simple language the answer to many of his problems.

To get the most out of this book it is suggested that you first read through the whole book at least once to familiarize yourself with the contents and to give you an idea of just what each chapter contains. Then, whenever a particular repair or project is begun, take time out before you start to read through the sections which apply. Even though you may be already familiar with the basic techniques involved, you may find that there are simplified methods described here which can save work or cut down on the cost of materials needed.

As in all reference-type books, the table of contents and the index should both be consulted. The table of contents is quite general and merely sets up overall categories where related information may be found. The index, on the other hand, is far more explicit, and in this particular book it is unusually complete. Since many of the tips and short cuts listed in one section can apply equally well to other problems, most items are cross-referenced under more than one listing or category. To find the answer to a particular problem, look under the key subject word. For example: If you have a problem with a leaking faucet, look under the word *Faucet*. If your problem is sticking drawers, look up *Drawers, sticking*. If you have difficulty finding the exact listing desired, try looking under the name of the tool or the materials involved or even the name of the particular technique or operation involved.

When turning to the page referred to by the index, you will find it useful to glance through the entire page, rather than just at the individual subheadings. Since subheadings must be necessarily brief, the material contained in each paragraph may cover more than one idea, and the index may be referring you to a paragraph whose title does not completely indicate everything it contains. In addition, since related short cuts are usually grouped together, you may find other helpful hints close by which will also be of assistance.

CONTENTS

HINTS and TIPS
for the
HANDYMAN

1

Use and Care of Tools

MAINTENANCE AND STORAGE

A Place for Everything

There is probably nothing that discourages a home handy-man faster than being unable to find a specific tool quickly when it is needed. Some kind of wall rack or storage system should be set up for all tools as soon as possible. Arrange tools so that all screwdrivers are together, all pliers together, etc. If lack of space does not permit putting up a regular workshop wall rack, then buy or build a tool box with compartments for all items. Do not simply throw everything together in one empty box. Sharp tools will be damaged, and small ones lost or misplaced.

Identify Tools

When working outdoors, the home handyman will frequently have small tools scattered around the outside on lawn or terrace. Make them all easier to spot by painting the handle of each one with a bright identifying color such as red or yellow. This also makes it easier for borrowing neighbors to remember where they came from.

Sharpen for Safety

Contrary to what some people think, sharp chisels, knives and planes are safer to use than dull ones. Dull tools may slip or gouge the work, and require extra pressure—all of

1

which makes them more hazardous to use. Keep tools sharp by honing edges frequently on an oilstone. Grind them only when the blades have been badly worn or nicked.

Storing Sharp Tools

To preserve the edge on chisels, gouges and other sharp tools build a small rack which holds them vertically with the tips or blades shoved into the top of a slab of synthetic sponge. The soft material will keep the blades from banging against each other, and also keeps the sharp blades covered so there is less danger of the handyman cutting himself.

Using Oilstones

When honing chisels or plane blades on an oilstone always place the blade so that the beveled edge rests flat on the stone (Fig. 1). Stroke the blade gently over the surface in

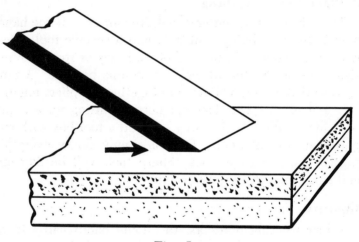

Fig. 1

a forward direction only. Do not draw it backwards since this will cause slight burrs or wire edges to form. Some old time craftsmen do work back and forth with an oval motion so that any burrs that are formed on the backward stroke are honed off on the next forward stroke—but this calls for greater skill and careful handling. Don't forget to keep the stone saturated with cutting oil to prevent clogging and to assure smooth cutting.

For a Keen Edge

Chisels are usually kept sharp by occasional honing on an oilstone. However, when nicks must be grounded out, or when extreme re-shaping of the edge is needed, then a grinding wheel must be used. Always grind carefully, taking off only a little at a time. Otherwise the blade may be entirely ruined. Let the blade cool after every three or four passes across the face of the wheel as hot metal has more tendency to chip. In extreme cases the temper may even be drawn from the blade so that it will not hold a sharp edge at all.

Sharpening Drills

When twist drill bits become dull they not only bore slowly they also are more hazardous to use and more prone to slip or wobble. Sharpening them is not difficult if an inexpensive grinding jig, which is sold for this purpose at all hardware stores, is used. These gadgets hold the drill bits at the correct angle for grinding, and enable you to put a keen, accurate edge on the bit in a matter of minutes.

Renewing Oilstone

Oilstones, used to put a final razor-sharp edge on knives, chisels and other tools, eventually become clogged with dirt, oil and old metal particles. To restore their original abrasiveness, fill a shallow pan with water and boil the stone in this till the old dirt is loosened up. If necessary, scrub with a stiff fiber brush and repeat the process several times until the stone is clean.

Handling Saw

Perspiration from the hands can cause steel saw blades and similar tools to rust rather quickly. To prevent this, avoid handling a saw by its blade whenever possible. In addition, always wipe both sides with a lightly oiled rag before putting it away after the job is done.

Protect Glass Cutter

Cutting wheels on glass cutters are easily damaged if they are allowed to bang around in a tool chest or drawer. To protect them slip a short length of rubber tubing over the cutting end before putting the tool away.

Sharpening Guide

When sharpening tools on a power-driven grinding wheel, the angle at which the tool is held against the surface of the wheel is all important if an accurate, smooth edge is to be assured. To provide a solid rest of exactly the right angle, cut a wooden block with a bevel at the top. Shape this bevel to hold the blade at the proper angle (Fig. 2). Take time out to make a separate block for each tool angle required so that in the future it will take only moments to sharpen each type of blade. Label the blocks clearly on the back so there will be no possibility of using the wrong one.

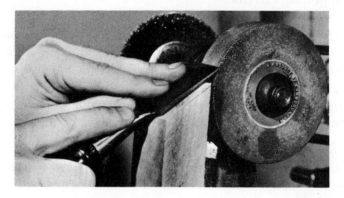

Fig. 2

Improvised Hone

A small strip of fine emery cloth tacked to the top of a block of wood makes an excellent hone for sharpening pocket knives and other cutting tools. Hold the tool blade at right angles to the length of the strip and move the edge sideways along the strip with light pressure. Replace the strip when it becomes clogged or worn.

Plane Blade

A properly sharpened plane blade can be easily nicked or dulled if the blade is left exposed when the plane is not in use. To protect the razor sharp edge from damage, the blade should be retracted when the plane is put away—or a strip of plastic adhesive tape can be pressed over the protruding blade.

Wood Bit Care

The lead-in screws on the tips of auger bits often become dull from contact with other tools in storage. To prevent this, use the manufacturer's trick. Screw each one into a bottle cork a little larger than the diameter of the drill so that the lead screw and cutting spurs are covered. This will prevent damage to all the cutting edges.

Circular Saw Blade Cover

To keep small saw blades from becoming nicked or dulled when stored in drawers or tool boxes, protect the teeth by stretching a wide rubber band cut out of a strip of old inner tube around the outside. This also protects the fingers against accidental scratching when the blade is handled.

Hacksaw Blades

Easily damaged hacksaw blades or coping saw blades can be stored and protected against toolbox abuse by wiping with an oily rag, then inserting in a length of aluminum tubing (available at hardware stores) about an inch longer than the blade length. Securely plug each end of the tube with a cork and you have an excellent damage-proof case for the blades.

Protect Blades

Power saw blades can be kept clean and rust-free if they are wrapped in heavy waxed paper before they are put away. For best results wipe the blade with a clean cloth to remove dirt, then repeat with an oily cloth to lightly coat the blade before wrapping it in wax paper. This system is also excellent for storing drill bits, chisels, and other sharp tools.

Saw Table Care

To keep the metal table on your power saw from rusting, and to keep it well lubricated so that rough pieces of lumber will slide more easily across its surface, a thin coat of paste wax should be rubbed on periodically. This will not stain the wood the way oil or grease does, yet it will still provide effective protection against corrosion.

Screwdriver Care

When a screwdriver blade starts to wear it tends to slip out of the screw slots easily. This makes it difficult to tighten screws securely and chews up the heads of tightly seated screws which must be loosened. To prevent this, the blade tip should be dressed occasionally by stroking with a flat file to eliminate rounded edges and to make the end blunt once more. Be careful to maintain the original bevel of the side faces and file across the tip at right angles so as to keep the blade end square (Fig. 3).

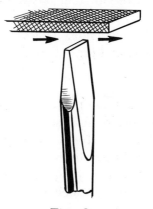

Fig. 3

Claw Hammers

When the claws on a claw hammer show signs of slipping every time a small-headed nail is pulled, try renewing their grip by filing the notch between them with a triangular file. Use a corner of the file to slightly deepen and sharpen the crevice between the claws. This improves their grip so they will "bite" the nail head more firmly.

Hammer Handles

Hammer handles sometimes work loose because the wood has dried excessively so that slight shrinkage occurs inside the metal socket. To swell the wood back up again and make it tight once more, soak the head end of the handle in a bucket of water for several hours. The handle can be kept from shrinking in the future by sealing the top end where it comes through the head with several coats of varnish or lacquer.

Pliers Care

When pliers accumulate dirt in the serrated teeth on the inside of their jaws they have a tendency to slip and will call for much greater pressure in order to hold. To correct this clean jaws out with solvent and a stiff wire brush, and re-sharpen individual teeth occasionally by dressing lightly with the edge of a three-cornered file.

For Easier Reading

Steel squares and other engraved metal rules often become difficult to read as they get older. For easier reading rub a crayon across the markings. Select one in a contrasting color. Then wipe off with a flat pad of cloth that has been moistened with a little kerosene or turpentine. The color will be wiped off the surface but will remain in the bottom of the grooved markings.

Cleaning Threads

Cleaning accumulated grease and dirt out of the threaded adjustment wheels on power tools is often a difficult job because it is so hard to reach into the grooves. Home craftsmen will find that an old toothbrush dipped into benzine or other solvent will do the trick nicely.

Drill Rack

One of the simplest ways to build a neat rack for drill bits of any size is to use a two or three-inch-thick block of hardwood for the rack. Use the bits themselves to drill the exact sized holes required. Store drill bits with the points down to protect against damage. To protect against rust the holes can each be saturated with a drop or two of oil.

Vise Jaws

A quick way to install new wooden jaws on the inside of your bench vise is to glue the blocks in place with contact cement. This adhesive is sold in all hardware stores and can be successfully used to glue wood-to-wood or wood-to-metal.

Hardwood jaws will last longest, but a soft wood such as pine will have less tendency to mar delicate work. When jaws have to be changed, the blocks can be removed by tapping with a chisel between the wood and steel.

Toolbox Tip

A small piece of rubber floor matting of the kind which is available at most hardware, auto or floor covering stores can be fitted into the bottom of a toolbox to prevent rattling and to keep tools from sliding around and banging together when the box is moved. The matting also prevents tools from coming in contact with rusty metal in the event the bottom starts to corrode.

Storing Chalk Line

A chalk line or plumb line can be easily and neatly stored by wrapping it around an empty adhesive tape spool. Snapping the spool into its original cover will keep the line clean, and will protect it against unwinding or tangling.

Storing Planes

When laying a plane down between jobs or for storage, never place the tool so that it rests on its blade. Either lay the plane on its side, or place it so that the front edge rests on top of a thin block of wood. This raises its front end sufficiently to keep the blade clear of the surface and protects it against nicking or dulling. (See Fig. 4.)

Fig. 4

PROPER USAGE

Sanding Machines

When electric sanding machines are used on furniture or cabinets only moderate pressure is required for fast, efficient cutting. On horizontal surfaces the weight of the machine is usually just about all the pressure needed. Handymen who bear down excessively only slow up the cutting action of the machine and will actually reduce its sanding speed and efficiency. In addition, there is the danger of overloading the motor.

Easier Sawing

Hand saws and hacksaws of all types will stay sharp longer and will cut with less effort if pressure is applied only on the cutting, or forward, stroke. Bear down firmly while pushing the blade forward, but lift up slightly when drawing it back. This avoids wearing down the cutting teeth needlessly.

Lubricate Saw

When hand saws are used for cutting through hard woods or gummy woods, they frequently bind or "grab," thus making the saw difficult to push. To ease the job, try rubbing a bar of soap along the teeth and on each side of the blade. The soap acts as an effective lubricant and keeps gum from sticking to the sides of the saw blade, but it will leave no stains on the wood.

Drilling by Hand

When holes must be bored with a hand drill, it is easier to keep the bit square to the surface if the drill is used in the horizontal position whenever possible. This simplifies sighting downward on the drill and prevents side-to-side deviations.

Keep Blade Clean

When tin snips and knives are used for cutting tarpaper or roll roofing, the black gum which accumulates on the blade is difficult to remove and interferes with efficient cutting action. To prevent this from happening, dip the blades in a pail of water between cuts. The water will keep the blade lubricated and will prevent the black tar or gum from sticking to the sides.

Drilling in Masonry

Carbide-tipped masonry drills sometimes show a tendency to "creep" away from their marked position when the hole is just being started. To prevent this, use a scrap of wood as a guide. Drill it with a hole to match the size of the bit and hold it over the spot where the hole is to be bored. The hole in the block will serve as a guide for the carbide bit and will help keep it square, while at the same time keeping it from creeping.

Easier Planing

When using a wood plane, the home handyman will find that it cuts smoother and easier if the tool is held at a slight angle to the cutting line as it is moved forward over the surface of the work (Fig. 5). This slight angle gives the

Fig. 5

cutting edge a slicing, or shearing, action which is much simpler to control than would be the case if the plane were pushed straight ahead with its cutting edge at right angles to the grain. Be sure to maintain a steady downward pressure at the same time.

Planing Edges

To prevent rounded corners at the beginning and end of a board when its edge is being planed, avoid rocking the plane by letting it dip over the far end of the piece or by letting it sag when you start the stroke. Either action will cause rounded corners at the ends. To prevent this, apply extra pressure on the front of the plane at the beginning of the stroke, and then apply extra pressure on the back end of the plane at the end of the stroke.

Star Drill Handle

Handling a star drill is uncomfortable work and often results in blisters and sore hands. A quick modification that saves hands is to wrap a number of layers of friction tape or masking tape around the drill shank to provide a slip-proof grip. The tape should be about one-eighth-inch thick. It will absorb most of the shock and vibration from the pounding.

Depth Gauge

When a number of holes must be drilled to the same depth with an ordinary electric drill, the problem of measuring the depth of each hole accurately can be an annoying and time-consuming chore. To speed the job considerably, wrap a strip of plastic tape around the bit at the height desired. Then drill each hole until the edge of the tape touches the surface.

Keep Chuck Key Handy

Many electric drill chucks require special keys to tighten them up. Keep this key handy by fastening it to the electric cord with a short piece of flexible wire or a heavy rubber band.

Testing a Level

If you are in doubt about the accuracy of your level, place it on the surface which you believe to be practically level and then note the location of the bubble in the glass. Now turn the level end-for-end and check the position of the bubble again. It should be in exactly the same position—in other words, it should have moved to the other side of the glass vial by exactly the same amount as it did the first time. If the surface used for testing is actually perfectly level, then the bubble should be precisely in the center no matter which way the level is placed.

Storing Nail Set

A nail set is always used with a hammer, so it is logical to keep them together. One easy way to do this is to bore a deep hole in the end of the handle· large enough and deep enough to permit the nail set to be slipped inside. It can be kept in place by plugging the hole with a small cork.

Correct Screwdriver

Home handymen should never use a single screwdriver for all size screws. The wrong size driver may chew up the screw heads unnecessarily, and may even ruin the tool itself. For best results, keep several sizes handy, and always pick the one whose blade fills the slot in the screwhead as much as possible. For most jobs around the home, three sizes (plus a Phillips-head driver) are all that will be needed.

Prevent Slipping

To provide a better grip for screwdriver blades, and to prevent slippage when heavy pressure must be applied, rub the tip of the blade over a cake of chalk beforehand. Ordinary blackboard chalk works fine.

Starting Screws

When a screw must be started in a hard-to-get at place it can be held with the end of the screwdriver blade if you will first fold a small piece of tape or paper over the blade before inserting it in the screw slot. Use enough thicknesses to permit wedging the blade in the slot, thus holding the screw in position on the end of the blade until it is started.

Cutting Tubing

Sawing thin-wall metal tubing with a hacksaw is often a difficult job because the blades tend to grab or chatter on the return stroke. Minimize this by mounting two blades in the hacksaw with teeth pointing in opposite directions. Then stroke lightly with even pressure on both forward and backward strokes.

Improve Miter Gauge

When mitering on a circular saw, home craftsmen often have trouble with work "creeping" or slipping along the polished face of the miter gauge. Avoid this by cementing a sheet of sandpaper to the face of the gauge with rubber cement. This will provide a nonslip surface against which the work can be held without difficulty.

Softer Grip

Use a small sponge-rubber ball to protect your hand when hammering on a cold chisel. Push the chisel through the soft rubber ball to provide a cushion grip for the hand while the tool is being struck with a hammer. It will absorb shocks and greatly lessen fatigue.

Measuring Trick

When using a steel measuring tape to make long measurements without the aid of an assistant, the hook end can be anchored in position by use of a small piece of plastic or cellophane tape. You can then stretch the other end as far as necessary without having to worry about the starting end slipping.

Keep Yardstick in Place

To keep long rulers or yardsticks from sliding around on the face of the work, glue small strips of fine sandpaper on the back at each end, and at intervals along its length. Use rubber cement so that the sandpaper can be easily peeled off when necessary.

JIGS AND ACCESSORIES

Emergency Drill

When necessary to bore a small hole in tight quarters where an ordinary brace or hand drill cannot be used, try using an ordinary door knob as a handle for the drill bit.

Slip the knob over the shank of the bit and tighten the set screw so that it grips firmly. The door knob will give sufficient leverage to enable you to turn the drill bit by hand and to bore through soft woods of moderate thickness.

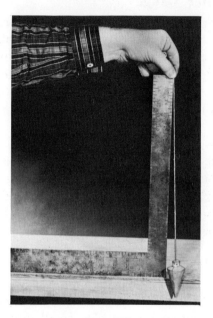

Fig. 6

Substitute for Level

In the absence of a level, a good substitute can be improvised from a steel square, a piece of string, and a plumb bob (Fig. 6). Place the square on the edge of the surface being tested as shown here. Then suspend the plumb bob (or other weight) at the end of the string. The surface is exactly level when the string is parallel to the upright leg of the square.

Tool Trays

Old bread pans and pie tins make handy tool trays which simplify the job of the home handyman when he has to make repairs away from his workbench or shop. All allied tools, hardware and parts can be carried in one or more trays to and from the job without danger of losing parts or forgetting needed items, and without the annoyance of trying to carry everything loosely in the hands.

Soldering Iron Holder

A wide-mouthed tin can such as a coffee can will make an excellent holder for a hot soldering iron. Cut notches in the top rim on opposite sides of the can so that when the iron is laid across the top it cannot roll off. Rolls of solder and cans of flux can be stored inside the can. (See Fig. 7.)

Fig. 7

Dust Brush

Home mechanics should save one of their small, worn-out paint brushes after it has outlived its usefulness for applying paint. Clean it as thoroughly as possible, then keep it handy around the workbench for dusting out corners and hidden crevices on woodworking projects.

Extra Blade

Save steps by always keeping an extra hacksaw blade or coping saw blade handy when working with these tools away from the shop. One easy way to do this is to tape an extra blade to the long side of the saw frame where it will be instantly available when needed.

Useful Knife

A handy knife for marking or cutting around the workshop can be made from a piece of an old hacksaw blade. A handle can be provided by placing a strip of wood on each side and then wrapping with friction tape or plastic tape. Leave about three or four inches of the metal protruding at one end· and grind the edge to form a sharp knife-like blade.

Holding Small Pieces

An adjustable wrench or locking-type pliers is ideal for firmly gripping very small pieces while drilling. Lock tightly onto the work and then clamp the wrench to the top of the drill press table or to a heavy wooden backing block. This can then be clamped in working position to hold the small piece safely.

Testing a Straightedge

To test the accuracy of a long board which you want to use as a straightedge, here is a simple method you can use. Lay the straightedge on a flat, smooth surface and draw a pencil line on the surface using the straightedge as a guide. Then turn the straightedge end-for-end, but with the same side still up and facing you. Place the board so that its original edge is again over the line just drawn. Its edge should now again match the line exactly. If it curves away at any point, then your board has a bend or curve in its edge.

Protect Metal Tubing

Thin-wall pipe or tubing is difficult to grip firmly in an ordinary vise without crushing or scratching it. Next time this comes up, try wrapping the tubing with a number of fine steel wool pads. These will provide a slip-proof grip which will hold firmly with a minimum of pressure between the jaws.

Rubber Handle

Anyone who has occasion to use a hammer a great deal will find that as his hands perspire the handle sometimes slips in his grip. To prevent this, wrap the handle with a layer of rubber electrician's tape or with adhesive tape. The grip provided will not only be slip-proof, it will also have less tendency to form blisters on the palms or fingers.

Miniature Vise

When working with small assemblies, or when tiny parts must be clamped together for soldering or for other ticklish jobs, an ordinary vise is sometimes too large and bulky to do the job properly. In such cases it will be found handier to grip the back of a C-clamp in the vise and then use the jaws of the clamp to hold the work instead. The clamp is easier to manipulate and the smaller jaws will be more convenient for holding small jobs. (See Fig. 8.)

Fig. 8

Cutting Sandpaper

When sheets of sandpaper have to be cut to size to fit sanding blocks or power sanders, they can be most accurately torn over a sharp metal edge such as the corner of a power saw table or other power tool top. Lay a ruler over the paper and snap the free end straight down for a clean, neat cut.

Foot Switch

A foot switch frees both hands for operating power tools such as drill presses and band saws. Such a switch can be inexpensively made by mounting an ordinary make-and-break push button switch (rated for 110 volts, 10 amps) on a wedge-shaped piece of 2 x 4. This holds the switch steady and raises it high enough to permit easy operation with the toe of one foot. The switch is wired in series with an outlet which is attached to the side of the block, and both are connected in series with an extension cord which plugs into a source of power. The tool is then plugged into the outlet at the side of the block.

Rubber Hammer

An ordinary hammer can be used instead of a rubber or plastic mallet when it is necessary to do light pounding on furniture or soft metals without damaging the finished surfaces. To convert a metal hammer for this purpose, slip a large rubber crutch tip over the head. These tips come in several sizes and are available at many drugstores or surgical supply stores.

Driver for Large Screws

To ease the job of driving long, heavy screws into hard woods—or for other heavy screwdriving jobs—home handymen should remember that special bits are available which can be fitted into an ordinary auger bit brace. Available in all sizes and equipped with square shanks so that they can be firmly gripped in the chuck, these screwdriver bits can be used in a brace when extra leverage is needed, or when speed is desirable because a large number of screws must be driven.

Eliminate Workshop Dust

To remove dust around the home workshop when doing a great deal of power sanding or sawing, put your wife's vacuum cleaner to work. Clamp or tie the nozzle of the cleaner beneath the power tool table. Have it running at the time sawing or sanding is going on. Sawdust will be sucked up promptly before it can spread to other parts of the house.

Fine Sawing

For a really smooth, fine cut when sawing small moldings and thin veneers use a regular metal-cutting hacksaw if you do not have a cabinetmaker's hacksaw. Select a fine-toothed blade and mount it so that the teeth cut on the forward stroke. A hacksaw also works well for cutting wood in a miter box when thin strips must be cut at precise angles and no standard fine-toothed saw is available.

Handle Comfort

Wire handles on heavy cans or pails can be uncomfortable to hold on to when they are fully loaded. To alleviate this problem slit a piece of garden hose and slip it over the wire handle. The result will be a broader, more comfortably cushioned grip that will eliminate sore hands.

Improvised Punch

Small punches for making holes in leather, rubber, cork, or cardboard are simple to make. Use metal pipe or tubing of the desired diameter. Cut off a three or four-inch length and place in a vise. File a one-half-inch-wide bevel around one end of the pipe until a sharp edge is created. Use the punch by hammering through the material which has been laid over a block of hard wood. This will make the punch easier to pull out, will give a clean cut, and will preserve its sharpened edge.

USING LADDERS

Protect Ladders

Wooden ladders will last longer if they are protected with occasional applications of clear varnish or penetrating sealer. Do not use an opaque paint. This might hide cracks or other defects so that it will be difficult to tell when the ladder becomes unsafe.

Non-Skid Steps

For a gritty, non-skid surface on ladder rungs, the home-owner can sprinkle fine sand over each one immediately after it is varnished. A less gritty surface will result if the sand is mixed right in with the varnish before it is applied.

Save Steps

Three or four half-inch holes drilled in the top platform of a stepladder will save much climbing to reclaim dropped tools while working on jobs requiring use of a ladder. The holes are used as a temporary rack to hold screwdrivers, pliers and the like. It keeps them handy in an upright position without the danger of their rolling off.

Protect Siding

When using an extension ladder on the outside of the house, the top of the ladder will sometimes mar siding or trip where it leans against the house. To prevent this, wrap the upper ends of the ladder with several thicknesses of heavy cloth. Or, you can also use a pair of old work gloves, slipping one over the top of each rail.

Carrying Stepladder

A heavy-duty drawer handle or screen door handle can simplify the job of carrying a stepladder from job to job around the house. Screw the handle to one of the vertical side rails (Fig. 9) to permit easier carrying of the ladder

Fig. 9

while it is laying down in the horizontal position. Take time to locate the handle at the center of balance so that the ladder will not tip when it is carried.

Prevent Slipping

To keep a stepladder from slipping dangerously on smooth polished interior floors, nail a pair of rubber heels to the bottom of each of the front legs. On metal ladders that do not have rubber feet the heels can be pasted in place with contact cement, used according to the directions on the bottle.

Support for Ladder

When a tall extension ladder must be used outdoors on soft ground, provide a firm rest for the legs by laying a short length of wide planking under the ladder ends. To keep the legs from slipping off the plank, nail a strip of scrap molding lengthwise along the plank's surface where it will act as a wedge under the ladder legs.

Ladder Tray

You can convert the top platform of any stepladder into a handy tray which will hold nails, screws, or tools without having to worry about their falling off. To do this, nail strips of quarter-round molding around the outside edge on top of the platform so as to provide a rim or low wall on all sides.

Ladder Safety

When using an extension ladder to reach high places remember to always set it up so that the base of the ladder is away from the base of the building by a distance equal to approximately twenty-five per cent the total height of the ladder. This makes for the safest angle and will prevent falling or slipping. In addition, never go higher than the fourth rung from the top when climbing.

Ladder Rest

To permit leaning extension ladders against the outside of the house where windows occur, a wide board of softwood can be nailed across the ladder at its top end to provide a "bridge" or brace. This will contact the window frame on both sides and will keep the ladder ends from touching the glass or screens. This board should be at least as long as the

Fig. 10

widest window frame likely to be encountered and about six inches wide. (See Fig. 10.)

Storing Ladders

Long extension ladders are usually stored by hanging on garage walls. This not only takes up a good deal of valuable wall space, it also requires a great deal of maneuvering each time the ladder is used. To simplify this problem and to save on space, the ladder can be easily stored on the garage floor by laying it down the middle directly under the car. The car can be driven right over it without interference, and a sheet of tarpaper will protect the ladder against oil drippings.

2

Handyman Techniques

MAKING HARD JOBS EASIER

Rust Removal

To remove small patches of rust from polished metals and tools, try rubbing the rusty spot with a hard typewriter eraser. The fine grit content of these erasers will polish out the rust, but will not scratch or otherwise damage the metal finish.

Renewing Putty

When putty that has been stored for some time is taken out of the can, it will often be too stiff to use easily. In most cases, kneading and slight warming will make it soft and pliable once again. Both can be accomplished by working vigorously between the hands. To avoid getting the hands oily and stained, place the putty in a plastic vegetable bag first. If the putty is exceptionally hard, a few drops of linseed oil placed inside the bag with the putty should do the trick.

Using Putty

Fresh putty has an annoying tendency to stick to the hands when used for filling nail holes in exterior woodwork, or for replacing a broken pane of glass. To prevent this, rub a little powdered whiting (available at all paint stores) or a little flour on the hands before starting.

Removing Damaged Screws

If a screw slot gets so damaged when the screw is part way out that it can no longer be gripped with the screwdriver blade, use a hacksaw to cut a new slot at right angles to the old one. A narrow-bladed screwdriver can then be used in this new slot, and will permit backing the screw the rest of the way out. Another trick that usually works is to grip the outside of the screwhead with a locking-type pliers, then use this as a wrench to turn the screw out of its hole.

Broken Screws

When a wood screw breaks off below the surface of the wood it is almost impossible to remove it without damaging the wood. Rather than trying to get the screw out, drive it deeper by hammering with a nail set. Then fill the hole with plastic wood and start with a new screw.

Headless Nails

Nails which break off at the head are always a problem to remove. One easy way to do this is to first grip the nail shaft securely with a lock-wrench type of pliers, then use a claw hammer under this to pull up on the pliers. Keep shifting the grip downward as the nail is pulled upwards.

To Bend Tubing

To bend metal tubing without causing kinks, first fill the tube on the inside with damp sand. Nail wooden blocks to the bench top to provide a form around which the tubing can be bent. Drain out the sand by tapping lightly with a wooden mallet after the job is done.

Locking Setscrews

If you are troubled by setscrews that continually work loose on V-belt pulleys of motor driven machines, you may find this trick handy. Remove the screw entirely and force a small piece of rubber (cut from a heavy rubber band) to the bottom of the hole. Then tighten the screw snugly once more. The compressed rubber at the bottom will maintain tension against the screw and will keep it from loosening in the future.

Matching Doors

When building cabinets which are to be covered with a pair of matching hinged doors on the front, here is a simple method for assuring that both doors will meet perfectly in the middle after they are hung. Fabricate the two doors as one piece, then saw them apart in the middle afterward (Fig. 11). This assures a perfect fit where they

Fig. 11

meet at the center joint. The width of the saw kerf will provide just the right amount of clearance needed to prevent rubbing or binding.

Sliding Cabinet Doors

When small sliding doors of hardboard or plywood are needed for cabinets, grooved tracks can be easily made without power tools. Use a length of the aluminum extruded material which is sold for this purpose in many hardware stores and lumber yards. It has grooves which are a perfect width for these materials, and it can be cut or drilled with ordinary tools. Double channels are available for bypassing doors, or two single channels can be screwed down alongside each other.

Accurate Measure

When necessary to measure the length of a piece of wood needed for an accurate fit between floor and ceiling, or between the inside walls of a closet or cabinet, the job can be done most accurately without use of a ruler. Use two wooden sticks, each a little more than half the length board needed. Butt one piece against the ceiling, and the other against the floor. Clamp them together where they overlap in the middle, using a C-clamp or similar device to hold them tight. When this is laid flat, it can be used as an exact measurement of the length board needed.

Old Moldings

When re-using old moldings which have nails in them, use wire cutters to snip off the old nails rather than hammering them out. This will save a lot of puttying of extra nail holes, and eliminates any possibility of splintering or cracking caused by driving the nail-heads back through the face.

Save Sawdust

When finishing hardwood cabinets or wall panels where a great deal of sanding is required, the wise handyman will save the sawdust and store it in glass jars or clear plastic containers. When mixed with glue and water later on, the sawdust makes an excellent crack or nail hole filler which will blend in perfectly with the natural wood.

Save Moldings

When prying off moldings which are to be saved and re-used, damage can be avoided by using a wide-bladed, stiff putty knife, wide chisel, or similar tool with a wide blade. Use of a screwdriver or other narrow tool will cause unsightly gouges and may ruin the molding by cracking it. Try to do most of the prying right next to the nails.

Space for Expansion

When putting up large sheets of wall paneling, the home handyman should avoid butting sheets together too tightly. A slight gap is necessary to allow for expansion and settling action later on. Besides this, sheets which are forced tightly together will often buckle or warp later on when pressure builds up due to natural expansion of the panels in humid weather.

Prevent Warping

When wide boards and large panels of plywood warp or buckle, the trouble is usually caused by one side absorbing more moisture vapor than the other. To prevent this happening, always try to paint or seal boards on the back side as well as on the front before assembling. This will make them uniformly resistant to moisture absorption on both sides so that they are much less likely to be damaged by warping.

Prevent Dents

When forcing tightly fitted pieces of finished wood together, avoid striking with a metal hammer since dents or other marks will result. A handy way to do this is to slip a rubber crutch tip permanently over the hammer handle end. The handle can then be used as a "persuader" for tapping or forcing pieces together by rapping sharply with the rubber-tipped handle end.

Save Parts

When working on small models or other assemblies which require that many small parts be sorted out and saved, the handyman will find that a piece of clear adhesive-backed cellophane tape can be used to keep pieces from being mislaid. Place a strip of the tape on the table, sticky side up, then put the parts on this. They will be held in order exactly as put down so that they can be quickly located when needed.

Save Bolts

When taking apart mechanical equipment or appliances which are assembled with bolts or screws, home mechanics can eliminate the possibility of misplacing the various bolts or screws if they will develop the habit of replacing each one in its original hole after the pieces have been disassembled. Not only does this minimize the danger of losing individual pieces, it also lets you know immediately where each bolt belongs when the parts are fastened back together again.

Man-Sized Thimble

When a handyman is faced with the occasional job of sewing canvas or other heavy materials which call for use of heavy needles, a thimble to protect the finger-tip can be quickly improvised from adhesive tape. Wrap several thicknesses around the finger, doubling it over several times at the point where pressure must be applied.

Eye Protector

To protect the eyes when grinding, chipping or scraping, a skindiver's face mask can be used instead of regular goggles. It wraps around and protects the eyes from the sides as well as below. The inexpensive toy versions which are sold for use by youngsters will do just as well as the more expensive versions.

Easy Marking

Felt-nibbed marking devices which are available at art supply stores and stationers can be used to write or mark on almost any type of material, including metal, glass or plastic. They come in various colors and are handy for such tricky jobs as numbering storm windows and screens, drawing lines on sheet metal before cutting, and putting identifying marks on switch boxes or tools. The markers can make anything from a fine line to a wide stripe, and dry to a permanent, waterproof finish in a matter of seconds.

Clip It On

A nail set is a frequently used tool whenever carpentry is being done. However, because of its size it is continually being misplaced or lost. To keep it always handy, slip an inexpensive pencil clip over the shank so that it can be easily clipped on to your pocket much like a fountain pen or pencil.

Reinforce Concrete

Old wire coat hangers can be used as an excellent substitute for reinforcing rods or wire mesh when pouring small concrete stepping stones or other odd-shaped forms. Bend them to the shapes desired, and tie together with short pieces of wire. Put in half the cement, lay the wire hangers on top, and then pour the rest of the cement over them.

Iron Edge

To increase the versatility of his workbench, the home mechanic can screw a length of angle iron to the front edge of his workbench (Fig. 12). This will serve three purposes:

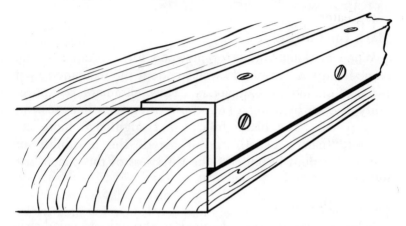

Fig. 12

(1) It keeps the front edge of the bench from becoming chipped or damaged. (2) It acts as a lip or raised edge which will prevent small parts from rolling off the table. (3) It serves as a handy anvil for bending or hammering when working on small metal parts.

CUTTING AND DRILLING

Cut Without Chipping

When cutting brittle materials that are subject to chipping (such as hard plastic laminates), always use a saw with very fine teeth and very little set. In most cases a hacksaw blade works fine. Hold the saw so that the blade is as flat as possible—that is, as nearly parallel to the face of the sheet as practical. Cutting with the blade almost at right angles to the surface will only increase the danger of chipping and will result in a ragged cut.

Duplicate Pieces

When a number of lengths of wood must be cut to the same size, use only one piece as a guide or measuring stick for marking off each of the other pieces. If the successive, freshly cut lengths were used each time, slight errors would be multiplied by each succeeding piece so that the last one might be off considerably. By using the same piece throughout, the possibility of compound errors is eliminated and greater accuracy will be assured.

Mark for Cutting

When marking lumber or plywood for accurate cutting, home handymen would do well to adopt the technique used by most skilled cabinetmakers. They eliminate the possibility of error by using a knife for scoring their lines instead of a pencil. The blade follows a straightedge more accurately than a pencil, and it avoids the possibility of minor variations because of the thickness of the pencil line itself.

Sawing Plywood

When sawing through plywood, or through old wood that is covered with a thin veneer, it is often difficult to get a clean cut without splintering. The top layer of veneer tends to lift with each stroke of the saw. Prevent this by first pressing on a strip of wide cellophane tape or paper gummed tape along the line of cut. Sawing through the tape will prevent splitting or lifting of the veneer and will result in a clean cut.

Fine Sawing

For fine cutting of small moldings and veneers, use a fine-toothed metal-cutting hacksaw instead of the usual rip or crosscut saw blade. Mount the blade so that the teeth cut on the forward stroke, and lift up on the blade as each backward stroke is made.

Prevent Binding

When rip-sawing a long board, the saw frequently binds because it becomes wedged in its slot. To overcome this annoying problem, wedge a large nail or screwdriver into the slot behind the saw. This relieves the pressure that causes the binding action. Move the wedge to keep it about one foot behind the saw blade.

Smooth Cut

Getting a smooth, even cut on thin pieces of metal or other thin materials is sometimes a problem. To guarantee a clean cut each time, place the material between two pieces of scrap plywood which are approximately as large as the material being cut. Then place this "sandwich" in a vise, or clamp tightly together, and saw through all pieces at one time.

Cutting Glass

For a smoother, crisper cut on glass always lubricate the wheel of the glass cutter by dipping it into some kerosene or turpentine before each cut. Use a straightedge to guide the cutter, and bear down with moderate pressure. Score the entire line in one swift stroke and avoid doubling back over the cut mark.

Cutting Glass to Shape

When sheets of glass must be cut to a particular shape or outline, draw the pattern beforehand on a sheet of paper in the actual size required. Place this pattern under the pane of glass so that the exact outline can be followed while you guide the wheel of the cutter over the top of the glass. When straight cuts are needed, use a wooden straightedge to guide the tool.

Enlarging Hole

To re-bore a hole in wood when a larger size opening is needed, a starting grip for the new, larger bit can be provided by first plugging the old hole with a scrap block of wood. Cut this block large enough to permit wedging it tightly in the hole. Then center the point of the larger bit on this and re-bore the new hole to the size desired.

Drilling Glass

When necessary to drill holes in bottles, jars, or other objects made of glass, try using a short piece of an old triangular file as a drill bit. Build a dam of putty around the spot where the hole is to be drilled, then fill this with turpentine. Sharpen the end of the file on a grinding wheel so that it forms a point, and use this in the drill chuck to bore the hole in the middle of the pool of turpentine. (See Fig. 13.)

Fig. 13

Boring a Clean Hole

To avoid splintering wood on the back side when boring a hole, place a scrap piece of wood behind the work before clamping it in a vise. Tighten the wood vise firmly and bore through both pieces. The result will be a clean bore through the work since only the scrap piece will splinter when the bit comes out the back.

Punching Pilot Holes

Instead of drilling individual pilot holes for small screw eyes or wood screws, time can be saved by punching holes in the wood with a fine nail set or with a common nail of the proper size. Hammer in only deep enough to give the screw thread a good start.

Angular Holes

When boring large-size holes in wood with an auger-type bit, difficulty is sometimes encountered in trying to get the bit started if the hole must be drilled at an angle to the surface. To help guide the bit make a small pilot hole beforehand at the proper angle with a narrow-gauge twist drill or an ordinary nail. The pilot hole should be smaller than the screw tip on the auger bit so that the point will take hold satisfactorily.

Drilling Sheet Metal

To ease the job of drilling clean holes in sheet aluminum or in other thin metal, try clamping the sheet between two pieces of scrap lumber first. Then drill through the wood and metal at the same time. The wood will keep the drill from grabbing and will eliminate rough, sharp edges around the hole.

SMOOTHING AND SHAPING

Smoothing Wood

Rough, porous boards can usually be smoothed down more easily prior to painting if sanding is done after a thin coat of shellac is applied rather than directly on the raw wood. Shellac should be thinned half-and-half with denatured alcohol and allowed to dry for about an hour. Then sand with fine grit paper, applying only moderate pressure and working parallel to the grain. Dust thoroughly before painting.

Mask Is Needed

When home handymen use an electric sanding machine to speed the job of sanding down large sheets of wall paneling, a mask should be worn to protect nose and throat against irritating dust. Good safety practice also requires that goggles be worn to protect the eyes. Both pieces of equipment cost only a few cents and can save a great deal of annoying irritation to sensitive parts of the nose and throat, and can prevent injury to the eyes as well.

Sanding Small Pieces

A sheet of sandpaper tacked to one corner of the workbench top comes in handy for sanding very small pieces. It is easier to hold such small objects in your hand and rub them over the paper than it is to sand the work in the usual manner.

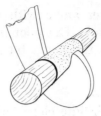

Fig. 14

Sanding Short Cut

When sanding the edges of inside curves or cut-out scroll work, the job can be made easier and the edges kept square if the sandpaper is first wrapped around a short piece of pipe or a heavy dowel (Fig. 14). The diameter of the pipe will depend on the radius of the curve being sanded.

Avoid Burns

When using an electric power sander or a sanding disc in an electric drill, make sure that only a moderate amount of pressure is applied. Also keep the sanding unit moving steadily at all times while the power is turned on. These devices all sand at a high rate of speed, and if allowed to stop in one place for too long will cause burning or scorching of the wood as well as gouging and pitting.

Fine Sander

A small emery board of the type women use in fingernail care can be a handy addition to the home craftsman's working kit. The emery board permits sanding in tight places where ordinary sandpaper or other abrasives will not fit, and it provides a ready-made, semi-rigid shaping tool for use where a fine-toothed file or scraper is needed.

Sandpaper Backing

When strips of sandpaper must be used to rub down round furniture legs or to work inside carvings, they tear quickly unless a cloth backed abrasive is used. In lieu of this, ordinary sandpaper can be used if it is first backed with strips of self-adhesive cellophane or cloth tape. The tape provides the reinforcement needed to keep the paper backing from tearing.

Sanding Grooves

A flexible, round sand block for sanding inside small grooves and moldings can be quickly improvised from a piece of rubber tubing about three or four inches long. When wrapped with a strip of sandpaper, it can be squeezed to the shape desired and run lengthwise along the groove or molding.

Smoothing Glass Edges

Exposed rough edges or freshly cut sheets of glass can be easily smoothed down with ordinary sandpaper wrapped around a block of wood. For a rounded or beveled edge, wrap the sandpaper around a small piece of foam rubber or a flexible sponge instead of the wood.

Planing End Grain

When the end grain of a board is being planed, there is always the danger of splitting off the corners as the blade goes past the edge. On wide boards this can be prevented by planing from either edge in toward the center, going no more than halfway across with each stroke. On narrow boards where only one-way planing is feasible, clamp a piece of scrap wood tightly against one edge. Run the plane from the good piece onto the scrap piece so that any damage done by the blade will be to the far edge of the waste lumber rather than to the good piece. (See Fig. 15.)

Fig. 15

For Easier Planing

To ease up on the sometimes difficult job of planing large, flat hardwood surfaces, here is an old trick used by many skilled craftsmen. Dampen the surface ahead of time by sponging it lightly and evenly with plain water. This will raise the grain slightly, and will give the edge of the blade a better "bite," particularly if it has also been freshly sharpened.

GLUING AND FASTENING

Avoid Excess Pressure

When clamping glued joints in woodwork, avoid tightening clamps excessively. Apply only enough pressure to bring parts in firm contact, and to hold them there while the glue hardens. Excessive clamping pressure will only squeeze out most of the glue so that the dry joint will be very weak. In addition, the pressure may warp or buckle pieces so that members will be permanently forced out of alignment.

Gluing With Shellac

Shellac is a well-known finish for wood, but most home craftsmen do not realize that it is also a powerful adhesive which is frequently used industrially. Use it thick and coat both surfaces to be joined. Allow to set for a few minutes till it becomes sticky to the touch, then press together. Shellac is especially good for cementing glass to glass, leather to metal, or leather to wood.

Glue Spreader

The problem of spreading glue over large flat surfaces, as when face-gluing two boards together, has always been a time-consuming and difficult job. The glue must be spread evenly yet quickly so that the usual small glue brush is hardly adequate. Next time this comes up, try using an old windshield wiper blade. The flexible rubber will spread the adhesive smoothly and will permit covering wide areas with a single sweep. For heavier cements or adhesives a short length of broken hacksaw blade can also be used. Held sideways, the teeth will work much like a notched trowel and will spread the cement on in a smooth, even layer of uniform depth.

Disposable Glue Brush

An inexpensive glue brush that can be thrown away after every job can be quickly improvised by simply twirling a swab of cotton around a wooden toothpick. Also good for very small touch-up jobs on painted surfaces, applicators of this kind can be purchased ready-made at most drug stores.

Larger Clamps

When the largest clamp available is still not wide enough to grip the work at hand, an extension can often be improvised by using two clamps in tandem. Hook the end of one clamp inside the end of the other, then open the screws as far as they will go. This will permit gripping work that is almost as wide as the combined capacities of the two clamps, or about twice what one clamp would handle. (See Fig. 16.)

Fig. 16

Gluing Joints

To squirt liquid glue into tight-fitting spots, special hypodermic-like injectors are available. In an emergency, a small rubber baby syringe can also be used. A syringe of this type also makes a handy applicator for spreading glue for ordinary jobs since a squeeze dispenses the glue and the top spreads it at the same time.

Doweling

When assembling wood joints that are glued and doweled, if the dowel is too snug to fit in the hole there will be no room for glue on the inside. To correct this, cut a groove along the length of the dowel before inserting it, or file a flat spot on one side to form a pocket which will let trapped air escape and provide room for the liquid glue.

Improvised Clamp

When gluing together drawers, chests, chairs or tables, an excellent temporary clamp can be improvised out of a length of rope and a stick of wood if no regular cabinetmaker's bar clamp is available. Wrap the rope loosely around the piece of furniture and use the stick to apply pressure by twisting it, tourniquet fashion, on one side (Fig. 17). To

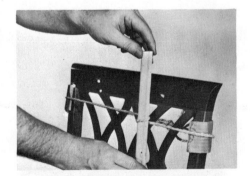

Fig. 17

protect the furniture, pad the corners where the rope squeezes with folded pieces of heavy cardboard or cloth. Tie the stick temporarily in position with an extra piece of string to keep it from unwinding and to maintain pressure until the glue has hardened.

Emergency Nut

When a nut has been lost or misplaced and another one of exactly the same size cannot be found, a nut of slightly larger diameter can often be used as a temporary expedient until a new one can be purchased. To make it fit securely, hammer the oversize nut slightly out-of-round by tapping it gently with a hammer while holding on edge on a hard surface. Forcing it out-of-round in this manner will usually make it grip the threads sufficiently to hold it in place under a moderate amount of tightening.

Prevent Damaged Threads

When a bolt must be shortened, thread a nut over the end before hacksawing it off to the desired length. Run the nut down past where the cut will be made so that the damaged threads near the end can be retreaded by simply unscrewing the nut after the cut has been made.

Locking Nuts

To prevent nuts from working loose, a few drops of clear shellac can be applied to the threads just before tightening. This will dry quickly and will prevent the nut from vibrating loose. The nut can be easily removed when necessary by applying a little extra pressure on the wrench.

Starting Brads

Small brads of less than one inch in length are difficult to start because your fingers usually get in the way as you try to hold them while the first blow is being struck. To solve this problem, try using a pair of narrow-nosed pliers instead of your fingers. In very hard woods punch a small hole first, using a finely pointed awl or an ice pick.

Coated Nails

One type of nail with which most handymen are unfamiliar is the coated box nail. These have a rosin coating which makes them hold and grip much better than conventional nails. They are particularly useful in edge-nailing when only thin nails can be used because of the danger of splitting. A thin, coated nail will hold in the end grain better than a much heavier uncoated nail.

Toenailing Aid

A rubber door wedge or doorstop can make a handy addition to any home carpenter's tool kit. When framing structures that require pieces of lumber to be toenailed in place, the door-stop can be held in place against the back side of the piece being toenailed. It will keep the wood from sliding out of position while the nails are being driven in at an angle on the other side. (See Fig. 18.)

Fig. 18

To Avoid Splitting

Certain types of lumber in the cheaper grades seem to split every time a nail is driven through them. One way to avoid this in most cases is to first flatten the point of the nail slightly by turning it upside down and tapping with a hammer. The blunt point will tear through the fibers of the wood and is less likely to cause splitting.

Driving Nails

Driving nails in hardwood is often tough going. To simplify the job try dipping the nails in linseed oil immediately before hammering. The oil will lubricate the nail and will make the job easier with less danger of bending.

Simplify Nailing

To facilitate starting nails in hard-to-reach spots where only one hand can be used, or on jobs where another hand is needed to hold the work, use a lump of putty or modeling clay. Press the wad of clay or putty onto the surface over the spot where the nail is to go. Pushing the point of the nail into this will hold the nail in place so that it can be started with a sharp blow from the hammer. The putty or clay can be removed afterwards.

Lubricating Wood Screws

A bit of paraffin, wax or soap rubbed over the threads of a wood screw makes it much easier to drive, particularly in hard woods. One way to keep this lubricant always handy is to drill a three-eighths-inch hole about one inch deep in the end of your hammer handle. Fill this with melted wax or paraffin and allow to harden. The screw can be twisted into this just before driving.

Screwing into End Grain

When screws are driven into the end grain of a board, their holding power is much less than if the screws were driven into the side grain of the board. When extra strength is needed, this holding power can be increased by first drilling through the board at right angles to the direction of the screw and directly through the path the screw will take. Fit a short piece of wooden dowel into this hole, positioning it so that the screw will pass through it when inserted (Fig. 19). This will insure a strong bite or grip

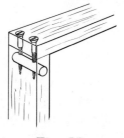

Fig. 19

which will be every bit as strong as if the screw had been driven into the side of the wood.

Screws That Rust

When screws that are not rustproof are used in assembling furniture, rust stains sometimes form around the screw holes because moisture has worked its way in. To prevent this happening, apply a few drops of varnish or shellac to the screw hole before inserting the screw. This will seal against moisture, and will also help prevent loosening.

3

Repairs and Improvements

EXTERIOR MAINTENANCE

Cracked Siding

Small cracks on outside siding or stucco often are not attended to because the homeowner mistakenly feels that these are not a serious threat to his house. However, they can permit surprisingly large amounts of moisture to enter. This causes eventual rotting of the inside timbers, and also attacks the siding from behind, where the wood is unprotected by paint. In stucco even more damage can result. The water freezes inside the crack in the winter and causes the crack to widen and the stucco to eventually buckle outward and fall loose. To prevent troubles of this kind before they reach serious proportions, always inspect the outside walls of your house at least twice a year. Fill the small cracks quickly with caulking compound. The job can be done with a putty knife, but a neater and more efficient repair will result if the caulking is squeezed in under pressure with a calking gun.

Working on Roof

When necessary to climb up on a roof to make repairs, always wear rubber-soled shoes. To give a firm footing on sharply sloping roofs, lay half of an extension ladder flat on the roof. Tie it at the top end to a chimney or pipe near the peak, or use a special roof hook which is sold for this purpose in most paint stores. These clamp onto the top rung of the ladder, and hook over the roof peak when the ladder is laid flat. In an emergency a rope can be tied to the top rung, thrown over the peak to the other side of the house, then tied to something firm (tree, window frame, etc.).

Roof Shingles

After heavy windstorms, homeowners who inspect their roofs may find that some roof shingles have been lifted up or curled back so that they no longer lie flat. This leaves the roof more susceptible to leaks since the next heavy rainstorm may blow water up under the shingles where it can seep down through the roof boards. To correct this situation, climb up on the roof and apply a dab of roof cement under each of the curled shingles so as to hold them flat. During the next warm spell, shingles will uncurl and will continue to lie flat even if the cement dries out.

Stepping-Stone Walk

An easy way for the homeowner to install a picturesque stepping-stone walk around the outside of his home is to cast individual concrete stones in place right in the soil. This avoids the necessity for lugging heavy stones and permits making each one any size or shape desired. Excavate the soil for each stone to a depth of about three inches, and make the sides and bottom of the excavation smooth and even. Then mix small individual batches of concrete for each form. Use the ready-mixed kind which is sold in bags in dry form so that only water need be added. Level off the top of each concrete stone by dragging a length of 2 x 4 edgewise across the surface. Allow to stiffen slightly, then rub smooth with a wooden float or trowel.

Anchoring Railings

When railings or other fixtures must be anchored to concrete floors or stoops, handymen can do the job best by using one of the special, quick-setting hydraulic cements that are available in most hardware stores or lumber yards. After the bolt hole is drilled (using a star drill or a tungsten-carbide bit), the bolt is placed head first in the hole with threads protruding. Then pour a freshly mixed batch of the hydraulic cement in around it. This cement sets up very quickly and very hard, and it expands tightly in the hole so that it grips permanently and securely. The grip will be improved if a washer is first slipped around the head of the bolt before anchoring.

Removing Efflorescence

The white, powdery stain that occurs on outside brickwork is unsightly in appearance and should be removed before paints or waterproof coatings are applied. Mix muriatic acid with four parts of water, adding the acid to the water (never the water to the acid) in a glass or wooden container—not metal. Wear rubber gloves, and scrub the solution on with a stiff bristle brush. Wait several minutes, then hose off with plain water.

Mortar Joints

Outside brick walls will develop damaging leaks if the mortar in the joints deteriorates to the point where it eventually falls out. To keep moisture out, mortar joints on all brick or stone walls should be inspected annually and repairs made immediately wherever defects are noticed. Scrape out the old crumbling or cracked mortar with an old chisel or large screwdriver and pack in freshly mixed patching cement. Be sure you dust out the crack thoroughly beforehand and dampen the brickwork with water.

Gutter Repair

To permanently repair rusted-out spots in metal gutters, first remove the rust on the inside by scrubbing vigorously with a stiff wire brush. Then spread on a liberal coat of roofing cement and cover with a sheet of heavyweight aluminum foil. Press down smoothly to eliminate air bubbles, then brush a second layer of cement over the top of the foil.

Fig. 20

Prevent Clogging

To keep downspouts from becoming clogged with accumulations of leaves and other debris which may be washed down from the gutter after a rainstorm, wire screens sold specifically for this purpose should be installed at the top of each downspout where it connects with the gutter (Fig. 20). These wire cage screens will keep leaves and other objects from falling down the drainpipe where they may eventually become wedged, causing water to back up in the gutter.

Basement Window

Below-ground basement windows surrounded by window wells usually become splashed with mud and dirt in heavy rain storms. To prevent this, dig out about three or four inches of soil and replace with an equivalent amount of clean gravel. This will prevent mud splashing up against the window and will also expedite drainage during wet weather.

Shingle Repair

For a quick but effective repair to prevent leaks through a split shingle, a square piece of ordinary tar paper can be slipped up underneath the shingle where it will be out of sight. This will keep water from entering until the homeowner has a chance to make a permanent repair by replacing with a new shingle.

Frozen Locks

During the winter, moisture may get into outdoor garage or tool shed locks and then freeze. This will make it difficult to insert the key and may make the lock impossible to open. When this happens, heat the key a few times by holding it in the flame of a lighter or match. Then work the key gently back and forth inside the lock. Repeat until the lock warms sufficiently to melt the ice inside.

Protecting Padlocks

When padlocks are used around the outside of the house, dirt, rust or other corrosion will sometimes form in the mechanism, making the lock difficult to open. To prevent this, place a strip of waterproof tape over the keyhole when it is not in use. The tape can be easily stripped off and replaced each time the key is inserted.

Outdoor Paneling

When building outdoor cabinets, storage boxes and other projects using plywood or hardboard, the home handyman should make certain he purchases only those grades designed for exposure to weather. Hardboard comes in a special tempered variety for outdoor use, and plywood comes in an exterior grade made with special waterproof glues.

Heavy Duty Scraping

For rough work where dried mud or hardened concrete must be removed from outside siding or trim—or where thick layers of blistered paint need scraping down—an emergency scraper that works well can be quickly improvised from a block of scrap wood and a small piece of metal lath or coarse mesh screen wire. Wrap the wire around the block and crimp at the corners to hold it in place, then rub over the surface. When the mesh becomes clogged, tap on a solid surface to clean it or replace with a new piece.

Rust Streaks

Rust stains on exterior painted siding are frequently caused by exposed nail heads which may be corroding beneath the surface of the paint. To correct this, sand off the nail head and spot-prime with a little shellac or a metal primer. Then countersink the nail head and fill the hole with putty before repainting.

Removing Metal Stains

To remove rust stains or other metal strains from light colored exterior siding, try washing with a water solution of oxalic acid. This is sold in crystalline form at paint and hardware stores. Dissolve three-quarters of a pound in one gallon of water and sponge over the stain. Allow to dry for several minutes, then rub off with a clean cloth.

Prevent Flooding

Water gushing out of a downspout during a heavy rainstorm cannot only wash out newly seeded lawns and flower beds, but it can also cause dampness in the basement and flooding of nearby cellar window wells. For effective drainage the water should be channeled away from the house foundation by means of underground drain tiles, plastic pipe, or a concrete splash pan at least three feet long. If a drain pipe is used, it can empty into a dry well, a drainage ditch or a nearby sewer. Concrete splash pans should be built so that the water empties onto a nearby sidewalk, driveway or other paved area where practical.

WINDOWS AND DOORS

Rattling Windows

Double-hung windows that continue to rattle even when locked can usually be silenced by driving two or three large rubber-headed tacks or rubber bumpers against the bottom edge of the lower sash (Fig. 21). Then when the window

Fig. 21

is closed, these will absorb the vibration and will take up the slack when the sash lock is closed so that adequate pressure will be maintained to prevent looseness.

Freeing Windows

In older homes windows that still have sash weights and cords can sometimes be freed up when they are stuck shut by trying this simple trick. Pull both cords out from the frame opening as far as they will go. This will raise the sash weights as far as they will go. Then let both cords go suddenly. The falling weights will frequently snap the frozen sash free when they hit bottom.

Binding Windows

Windows that do not slide easily may simply be in need of a little lubrication. Dry soap, wax or paraffin rubbed in the tracks will usually do the trick. First, be sure to sponge off all dust or dirt and scrape away heavy accumulations of paint.

Loose-Fitting Windows

Windows in older houses often fit very loosely because the wood framework or the sash has shrunk so much that an excessive amount of space is left between the sliding sash frame and the moldings that hold it in place. This permits cold drafts to enter and may cause rattling. To remedy this condition, inside stop moldings should be carefully pried off with a chisel and then renailed after moving them slightly closer to the face of the sash.

Measuring Pane

When measuring for a piece of glass to replace a broken pane, remember always to have the glass cut approximately one-eighth of an inch smaller than the wood frame in both length and width. This allows for possible expansion or contraction of the wood and also permits bedding the glass in putty for a more airtight seal around the edges.

Broken Glass

When removing broken pieces of window glass prior to installing a new piece, avoid cuts on your hands by wearing heavy work gloves or by wrapping the broken slivers with heavy cloth to pull them out. Rock pieces back and forth gently, and then try to lift them straight out in one piece if possible. The old putty can then be pried out with a dull chisel. Be careful not to gouge or chip the wood.

Soften Putty

When the paint surrounding it need not be protected, hardened old putty on windows or other surfaces can be quickly softened up with lacquer thinner. Mop on a liberal coat, then wait a minute or two. It will soften rapidly so that the knife can easily scrape it out. But remember, the lacquer thinner will soften up any old paint with which it comes in contact, so keep it off surrounding surfaces if you don't intend to repaint.

Applying Putty

When spreading putty around a pane of glass while glazing windows, the job can be speeded up by first rolling the putty into long strips. Make each strip about as big around as a pencil, and press each one into position against the glass with the fingers. Then smooth with a putty knife.

Storing Putty

When a small amount of glazing putty remains in a partly used can it can be kept soft by scooping it out of the can and wrapping tightly in sheet plastic or in a plastic vegetable bag. This keeps out air and protects it against drying out. The putty can then be kneaded and softened before using while it is still in the bag.

Cold Weather Glazing

The homeowner who breaks a window during cold weather will have difficulty replacing the broken pane because of the stiff consistency even fresh putty will have when used outside. To soften the putty, heat a large stone or brick and lay the putty on it while working. This will keep it soft and oily and will assure easy workability until the job is done.

Screen Cleaning

Late winter or early spring is the time when homeowners should take out their screens, clean off the wire and coat them if necessary to prevent future corrosion. Scrap pieces of carpet are excellent for this job. Nail to blocks of wood for easy handling. Use one piece to dust the wire, another to apply screen enamel or varnish to the wire mesh. Discard each one as it gets dirty or worn.

Stretching Screen Wire

When new wire mesh is to be installed over window screens, handymen often have difficulty in stretching the wire tight. One easy way to do this is to lay the screen down so that it is supported only on its ends across the top of two wooden saw horses or chairs. Tack one end of the wire in place and roll the wire across to the other end. Then have an assistant bow the frame downward slightly (or use a heavy weight such as a pipe) in the middle about one inch and tack the other end in place (Fig. 22). When

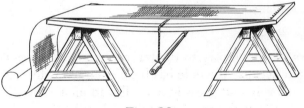

Fig. 22

the frame snaps back into the flat position, it will have stretched the wire mesh tight and smooth without effort. The sides are tacked down afterwards.

Protect Window Screens

Copper screening eventually oxidizes and causes green, rust-colored stains to run down onto the siding or woodwork. To prevent this, the wire should be cleaned annually and then coated with a clear spar varnish. One of the easiest ways to accomplish this job is to use varnish in an aerosol-type spray bomb. Stack screens up behind each other two or three at a time, and spray through all at once. Then turn them around and spray from the other side.

Screen Repair

Holes less than one-half inch across in screen wire can usually be plugged effectively without tiresome weaving and without use of unsightly large wire patches. Use clear fingernail polish dabbed on in successive layers until the hole is covered. Since the polish dries very quickly, several applications can be applied in rapid succession.

Doors That Bind

When doors that have been operating satisfactorily suddenly start to bind and refuse to close smoothly, the first thing the homeowner should suspect is loose screws in the hinges. Swing the door wide-open and test all screws with a large-headed screwdriver to make certain that they are firmly seated. If some turn freely no matter how much they are tightened, it is an indication that the threads have been stripped in the wood behind it. To remedy this, completely unscrew one side of the hinge and refill the screw hole with wooden slivers so that the screw will once again hold tightly when replaced.

Loose Screws

Another quick way to tighten up hinge screws which will not hold because the hole has been enlarged is to remove the screw entirely and press in a small wad of steel wool. When the screw is replaced, the steel wool will take up the slack so that the screw once again grips firmly.

Sticking Doors

Before doing any planing on the edge of a sticking door, make certain you know exactly what areas need to be shaved down. To determine this, use a piece of ordinary carbon paper. Slip it over the edge of the door at various points, and then close the door over it. Black smudges on the door will indicate the exact spots where rubbing occurs.

If It Rubs at the Bottom

A door that rubs slightly at the bottom each time it is swung open or closed can often be cured without planing. Try laying a sheet of coarse sandpaper on the floor or saddle at the point where the door rubs. Work the door rapidly back and forth over this sheet of sandpaper a few times. This will usually remove just enough wood to stop the binding or scraping.

Lubricating Hinges

Ordinary pencils have leads made of graphite and can be used in an emergency to lubricate squeaking hinges and other slow-moving parts. Pull out the hinge pin and rub the pencil lead over the outside of this pin before reinserting it. The graphite will lubricate it sufficiently to permit freer action and will eliminate squeaking.

WALLS AND CEILINGS

Fine Cracks

When very fine hairline cracks occur in plaster ceilings or walls, they can be filled in effectively without use of spackle or plaster by using ordinary sticks of white chalk. Rub vigorously back and forth over the crack till it is filled in. On white ceilings this forms an excellent temporary repair which will need no further touching up until time for the next paint job.

Plaster Patches

When using plaster to repair deep holes in walls or ceilings, always apply in layers rather than in a single application. Apply no more than a one-half-inch thickness at one time, and allow each layer to harden before troweling on the next coat. The final layer should be built up slightly higher than the surrounding surface to allow for shrinkage. It can be sanded smooth and flush with the rest of the wall or ceiling after it has thoroughly hardened.

Bottomless Holes

A hole completely through a plaster or gypsum board wall is difficult to fill because there is nothing behind it to back up the patching material. One simple way to solve this problem is to cut a piece of heavy cardboard slightly larger than the size of the hole, but of such a shape that it can be slipped through the opening at an angle or by slightly bending it. Punch a hole in the center of this cardboard and push a large common nail through from behind. Slip the cardboard into the hole and, using the nail as a handle, hold the cardboard in place while some quick drying plaster is smeared across the front and around the edges of the hole (Fig. 23). Hold steady for a few minutes until the plaster

Fig. 23

begins to stiffen, then you can let go. Allow to dry hard, then continue filling in the patch with additional layers of plaster. The nail can be pushed through so that it falls down inside the wall before the patch is completed.

Smoothing Patches

For a glass-smooth finish when patching plaster walls, allow the patch to set until the plaster begins to stiffen. Then dip the putty knife or trowel in water, and drag the wet tool over the surface of the partially hardened plaster. This will leave it with a smooth, glazed surface which will need little or no sanding.

Crack Cutter

When cracks in plaster walls or ceilings are repaired, it is important that they first be cut out (deeper and wider) so that a good mechanical bond will be assured when the patching material is applied. One of the handiest tools to use for this job is an ordinary puncture-type beer can opener. Its V-shaped blade and bent-over point gives it exactly the right shape for the task and makes it easy to hold.

Ready-Mixed Spackle

A prepared spackle eliminates the need for mixing powdered compound with water each time a little is needed for repairing small cracks. A putty-like mixture with exactly the right consistency for immedate use, prepared spackle is available at most paint stores in tubes as well as in cans.

Drilling Plaster

When drilling small holes in plaster walls, ordinary bits dull rapidly and may be completely ruined. A disposable bit can be improvised at little expense from an ordinary nail. Simply cut the head off and insert in the drill chuck with the point sticking out. This "throw-away" bit will drill holes cleanly without chipping, and will last for at least six or eight holes before it has to be discarded.

Catch Plaster Dust

When drilling holes, cutting cracks, or making other repairs to plaster walls and ceilings, the fine white dust created is difficult to clean up. To ease this job, place a double layer of paper on the floor directly underneath where you are working. Dampen the top sheet with water as this will catch and hold the dust better. Peel it off when it starts to dry or becomes loaded, and be careful to avoid walking on it.

Prevent Cracking

To keep plaster walls from cracking when driving in nails or picture hooks, place a strip of adhesive backed cellophane tape over the spot first. Then carefully drive the nail or picture hook through this.

Mixing Container

For mixing small amounts of patching plaster or spackling compound, cut a large rubber ball in half. Each section will then make an excellent mixing container, which can be easily cleaned by squeezing flat or by turning inside out if necessary.

Wallboard Joints

When walls of gypsum board are being put up, home handymen often have difficulty in getting a smooth joint or

seam where panels meet. Directions furnished usually recommend use of a wide putty knife or spackling knife to
apply the final coats of cement. However, the joint cement
will be easier to "feather" out along the seams if a conventional plasterer's trowel is used rather than a putty knife.
After a little practice the handyman will find that the trowel
is faster to use. It has a much wider blade, which will bridge
across the face of the seam in one stroke, and will simplify
smoothing the cement flush with the surrounding surfaces.

Nailing Wallboard

For countersinking nail heads when putting up gypsum
board walls, a ball-peen hammer makes an excellent tool.
Drive the nail till it is almost flush with the surface with your
regular claw hammer. Then place the ball side of the ball-
peen hammer against the nail head. Strike the flat side of
the hammer head lightly with the other hammer.

Nailing Studs

When toenailing 2 x 4 studs in place in order to frame out
a wall, it is often difficult to keep the piece being nailed into
position from slipping. One easy way to accomplish this is
to drive an extra nail directly behind the stud as shown in
Fig. 24. This need only be driven in for an inch or so to
keep the wood from slipping, and it is easily pulled out
afterward.

Fig. 24

Prevent Buckling

When sizeable construction projects are planned on the inside of the house, lumber and wall paneling should be bought well ahead of time and stored inside the room in which it will be used. This will give the wood a chance to dry thoroughly, and will minimize the possibility of any buckling or shrinking later on after pieces have been cut to size and nailed in place. With most lumber, one week's storage at normal room temperature will usually be sufficient.

Tile Joints

When the white mortar joints between individual bathroom tiles start to crumble or crack, repairs can be made with specially prepared grouting materials which are available for this purpose at most hardware and paint stores. However, before it can be successfully applied, the old material should be scraped out for at least one-eighth of an inch in depth. Then smooth in the new material and wipe off excess immediately with a piece of cloth wrapped around one finger.

Condensation Problem

Excessive moisture and humidity trapped in tightly built homes during the winter can cause a great deal of damage when it condenses inside cold outside walls. At least once a day open the windows about one inch at the top on opposite sides of the house for two or three minutes. The amount of heat lost will be negligible, but the amount of destructive water vapor that will escape can be sizeable.

FLOORS AND STEPS

Loose Boards

Floors that creak because boards are loose can be permanently cured by nailing upward into the subflooring from below. However, when this is impractical the squeaks can also be stopped by driving cement-coated finishing nails at a 45-degree angle from above. Nails are driven through the floor boards and into the subfloor from both sides so that they fasten down both edges of the offending boards. To conceal the repair, countersink nail heads slightly and fill with wood plastic in a matching color.

Squeaking Floors

Minor floor squeaks can often be eliminated with a dust-type graphite gun such as is commonly sold in hardware stores for lubricating door locks. A little of the graphite is squirted between the loose, creaky boards. This lubricates them where they rub and usually stops the squeaking noise.

Sagging Floors

When floors start to sag in any part of the house, the condition can be corrected by gradually jacking up the floor beams from below. For this job a steel jack-post or adjustable lolly column is needed. These posts are sold by large hardware stores and by most lumber and building materials dealers. They have a built-in screw jack at the top end. Place one under each of the sagging floor beams and raise gradually, a fraction of an inch per day, until the floor is level again. These posts must rest on top of a solid concrete floor, or on special concrete piles or footings poured in place for just this purpose.

Tongue and Groove

When nailing down tongue-and-grove flooring, it is often difficult to force the boards tightly together so that joints are snug. Simplify the job by using a small scrap piece of the same lumber. Place the scrap's groove over the tongue of the board that is being put in place. Hammering on the tongue side of the scrap piece with a hammer will force the board in place without damaging its tongue edge.

Removing Board

When a single board must be removed from the center of a floor which is covered with tongue-and-groove flooring and then replaced with a new one, here is the method to follow if you don't want to rip up the whole floor. Use a sharp chisel and hammer, or a power saw, to remove the defective board. Split it out in sections, working carefully so as to avoid damaging adjoining boards. Cut a new length for a snug fit, and then trim off one half of the grooved side on the bottom as shown in Fig. 25. Then the piece can

Fig. 25

be neatly dropped in place from above. Slide it in at an angle so that the tongue edge meshes first, then tap the grooved side down with a block of wood and a hammer.

Baseboard Molding

As floors in older houses settle or shrink, baseboard moldings are frequently separated from the floor so that an annoying dust-catching crevice is created underneath. To correct this, pry off the baseboard molding, remove nails, and then nail back down by driving nails in at a vertical angle so that they hit the flooring itself rather than the baseboards. This will assure that if any further settling or shrinking takes place, the molding will shift with the floor so that no more unsightly gaps appear.

Spreading Adhesive

When adhesives must be spread for application of floor tiles, make certain the correct tool is used. Most manufacturers recommend special notched spreaders or trowels which have notches cut to specific dimensions. These apply exactly the right amount of adhesive and will avoid the danger of putting on too much or too little. Also make certain to check the manufacturer's recommendation for the correct adhesive to be used.

Laying Tile

When putting down an asphalt tile floor in cold weather, it is important that the tile, the room, and the floor be warmed to at least 70 degrees if the tile is to lie flat. Stubborn tiles that pop up at the corners can be put down permanently by heating them lightly with an infrared lamp for a few minutes. Be careful not to leave it on so long that it scorches the tile. An electric iron can also be used.

Removing Damaged Tile

To remove one or two asphalt tiles from a finished floor without damaging those adjacent to it, use an ordinary electric iron. Lay a sheet of paper over the damaged tiles to protect the iron, and then heat thoroughly until the tile becomes soft and pliable. It can then be easily pried up with a wide putty knife after one corner has been cut away with a sharp knife.

Fitting Floor Tiles

To fit floor tiles around odd-shaped projections or corners, use a piece of flexible wire solder as a template. Press the wire into the corner until it conforms to the exact shape required. Then lay the wire form over the tile and trace in the outline to be cut.

Miniature Roller

To press down the edges of floor tiles when they are being laid, you will find that a large caster will serve as a handy little roller. Make a handle for the caster by drilling a hole in a scrap length of wooden pole or old tool handle. The caster is also ideal for use in tight corners on flooring where a regular roller might not fit.

Linoleum Repair

To patch holes in linoleum surfaces which have worn through or broken off, a mixture of powdered cork and clear shellac can be used. Using an ordinary food grinder, chop the cork as fine as possible, then mix with shellac until the consistency of thick paint is achieved. Trowel into the hole, allow to dry, then touch up with paint to make the patch as inconspicuous as possible.

Lifting Old Floor Tiles

When sections of an old tiled floor must be lifted, the job can be speeded up considerably by first covering the damaged tiles with a quantity of dry ice wrapped in a folded cloth. After an hour the tiles will become so brittle that they can be easily cracked and lifted off.

Cellar Stairs

Cellar steps can be a hazard at night, especially if the cellar is insufficiently lighted. To protect family and guests, try painting a one-inch stripe of luminous paint along the edge of each step. The paint will show up in the light, and will glow for protection in the dark.

Prevent Slipping

To provide a skid-proof surface on porch or cellar steps, sprinkle fine sand on just after a fresh coat of paint has been applied. An even better method consists of mixing the sand directly into the paint. Stir vigorously at frequent intervals to prevent settling and thin slightly to simplify brushing.

Basement Floor Repairs

When concrete basement floors are to be covered with tile, the homeowner often finds there are shallow depressions and rough spots on the surface. If not smoothed over, these will give the floor a wavy uneven surface that will be difficult to cover properly, thus spoiling the appearance of the finished job. High spots can be smoothed down by chipping away with hammer and cold chisel. However, shallow depressions must be filled in. Ordinary patching cement will not stick well in thin layers. For this job use one of the latex-cement combinations which are sold in many hardware stores and by dealers who specialize in floor coverings. These are used exactly like ordinary cement, but they can be applied as thin as required since they have a smooth, creamy consistency when mixed according to directions. Latex-cement is applied with a trowel or a wide spackling knife in much the same manner as patching materials are applied to a plaster wall.

4

Painting and Wood Finishing

BEFORE YOU START

The Right Paint

When shopping for paint, always specify clearly the job
for which it is intended. Indoor and outdoor paints both
come in a great many different types, and many are for-
mulated to handle only certain jobs and are to be used only
over specific surfaces. Don't make the mistake of thinking
that one paint can be used for everything. Ask questions of
the dealer, or read the manufacturer's label and other literature carefully. This is the only way to make certain that the
right material has been selected and that it will be properly
used.

The Right Tool

Paint brushes come in many different sizes and styles, but
the home handyman will find that he can do practically all
of his work with only three: a 1½-inch sash brush for windows and moldings; a 2½-inch trim brush for furniture,
woodwork and the like; and a 4-inch wall brush for a large
flat surfaces such as flush doors, outside walls and porch
floors. Rollers will generally be faster and easier to use on
interior walls and ceilings.

Selection of Bristle

Though brushes made of natural hog bristle are more expensive, and are best for fine varnishing or enameling, lower

priced nylon bristle brushes are best for use with water-thinned paints. The nylon bristles will stand up better than the hog bristle since they are not absorbent and are less likely to become flabby or tangled. However, for a smooth job be sure you purchase one of the better quality nylon brushes with bristles that have been artificially flagged or tipped (Fig. 26).

Fig. 26

Clean First

Even over the best prepared surface, paint has a difficult job adhering properly because of the beating it must take. Moreover, the film is weakened considerably if it cannot "grab" onto the surface. Grease, dust and other foreign materials will interfere with good adhesion and may cause premature cracking or peeling. To prevent this, never apply paint over a dirty surface. Wipe first with solvent or detergent, particularly in kitchens, bathrooms or other areas which normally get hard wear.

Thorough Mixing

Many home painters do not realize that unless a paint is thoroughly mixed its qualities—and even its color—may vary considerably from the top of the can to the bottom. For example, when low luster paints are not thoroughly stirred, the top part of the can may actually dry to a high gloss because all pigment has been left on the bottom. To prevent mishaps of this kind, paint must be thoroughly stirred until it is of uniform consistency from top to bottom. When opening a new can, never attempt to do this in the original container. Instead, pour half the paint into a separate can, stir the remainder thoroughly, then pour both halves together again and stir once more. Then pour the material back and forth a few times before starting to work.

Prevent Smearing

When painting doors, windows and other pieces of woodwork, the amateur painter often has difficulty in keeping paint smears off the ornamental hardware. To eliminate this problem, smear a thin coat of vaseline jelly over the metalwork before beginning to paint. Then if paint does get smeared onto the hardware, it can be easily wiped off with a rag afterward.

Not for Outdoors

Clear shellac is a versatile product which has many uses in indoor painting and wood finishing. However, it should never be used outdoors as a primer under varnish or other clear finish, or as a finish by itself. It turns white quickly when it comes in contact with even a moderate amount of moisture.

Remove Wax

Paint, varnish and other finishes will not dry properly when applied over surfaces that have been previously waxed. Handymen should remember to always clean surfaces thoroughly beforehand, using turpentine or a special surface preparer sold for just this purpose in almost all paint stores.

Head Covers

Free caps are available at most paint and hardware stores for protecting the hair when working overhead. However, many homeowners forget to ask for them and are all ready to start work before the need for one is remembered. To save making another trip, fold up a paper hat out of newspaper, much as the youngsters do when they are playing soldier. It will protect the hair from paint drippings and dirt, and can be discarded when it gets dirty.

Straining Paint

A piece of old nylon stocking makes an excellent strainer for paint. Tie a double thickness over the mouth of a clean paint pot by wrapping string around the top just below the rim. Let the nylon material sag slightly in the middle to form a sort of well. Then pour the paint into the center and let it drip through. Stirring with a smooth stick or the tip of a paint brush will help speed up the process. (See Fig. 27.)

Fig. 27

Tube Colors

Home painters who keep tinting colors on hand for mixing paints will sometimes find that partly used tubes have separated into paste and oil after they have been stored for some time. To prevent getting a blob of loose oil when the tube is first opened, leave the cap on and knead the whole tube lightly before opening it. This will mix the ingredients back together again. Storing upside down will also help, but make certain caps are on tight.

Smooth Patches

When using spackling compound or patching to fill large holes in walls or ceilings before painting, always apply the material so that it is a bit higher than the surrounding surface. This allows for the slight amount of shrinkage which often occurs and will enable you to sand it flush after it has thoroughly dried.

Odorless Paints

Many companies now manufacture interior paints that are very low in odor or completely odorless. These make indoor painting more pleasant for everyone. However, to keep them odorless, homeowners should purchase the special odorless thinner which is also available. Adding ordinary turpentine or other regular solvent will merely replace the odor that the manufacturer has removed.

Save Hardware

Before painting kitchen cabinets, remove all hardware from doors and drawers if you want to assure a professional-looking finish. Not only will this make the actual painting go faster and easier, it will also provide an opportunity to do a polishing job on the metal before replacing it.

Protect Fixtures

Before starting to paint any ceiling, loosen the base plates on all lighting fixtures so that they can be dropped down a few inches. Drape the fixture with an old cloth or a large sheet of paper to protect it against paint spatters.

Repair First

Before the outside of your house is painted, all necessary steps should be taken to eliminate any possibility of moisture entering the walls behind the new paint film. Check for and correct such defects as roof leaks, clogged gutters or downspouts, cracks in siding, missing caulking, open joints in siding or trim, and loose or dried up putty on windows. Otherwise, these defects may allow water to work its way into the wood behind the paint film and will eventually cause blistering and peeling.

Protecting Paint

Wet paint on the outside of the house has an annoying habit of attracting gnats, flies and other small flying insects. They stick to the surface and can often mar the otherwise attractive appearance of a finished job. To prevent this, add two tablespoons of citronella oil to each gallon of paint while mixing it. This oil repels most insects and will thus protect the finish.

Prevent Bleeding

Knots and sap streaks in raw wood should never be painted over unless they are first sealed. They will otherwise bleed through in a short while, leaving an unsightly brown stain which will show up even after several coats of paint have been applied. In addition, cracking or peeling will eventually result. To prevent this, touch up all knots or sap streaks by coating with shellac or a special knot sealer before paint is applied. This method of sealing also works well over old surfaces that have already been painted.

Eliminating Mildew

When painting over old surfaces where mildew is present, always take steps to prevent the fungus from returning before applying a new coat of paint. Treat the area first by wiping on a mild solution of household disinfectant or bleach. Then scrub thoroughly with a powerful detergent such as trisodium phosphate. Rinse clean and allow the surface to dry before painting. As an added precaution, a mildew preventive should be purchased from the paint store and added to the new paint before it is applied.

Pour Without Splashing

When pouring liquids such as turpentine or shellac from a square can which has its opening in one corner, hold the can so that the opening or spout is at the top when the can is in pouring position (Fig. 28). Air will be able to enter

Fig. 28

freely above the liquid giving a steady, easy-to-control stream which will not gurgle or splash.

Painting Trim

When purchasing white paint for the exterior trim on his house, the homeowner should make certain he specifies a sash and trim paint if the body of his house is dark in color. Ordinary chalking-type or "self-cleaning" paints may stain the dark walls below as exposure causes the old paint to chalk off. Exterior trim paints dry hard and do not wear down in this manner.

Painting Galvanized Metal

Paints will quickly peel off ordinary galvanized metal unless the surface is first properly treated. Sponge on some ordinary vinegar and let stand for about one hour. Then rinse off with plain water and let dry thoroughly before painting.

Battle Against Rust

Though paint protects metal against rust, paint itself can also be attacked because rust can creep underneath a paint film once it gets a chance to start on any exposed area nearby. As it spreads, the rust eventually lifts up the paint above it and causes peeling. To combat this, touch up all scratched or nicked spots as soon as noticed, and always clean down to the bare metal by rubbing with sandpaper or steel wool before new paint is applied. Use a metal primer as a base coat and allow to dry thoroughly before applying the top coat.

Check Dried Color

Paint changes color when it dries, so when mixing colors be sure to let a sample dry to make certain of the final shade. To save time smear a small sample of the paint on a piece of glossy cardboard. Lay it over a radiator, a lamp bulb or an upturned electric iron for a few minutes. This dries it quickly so that a true color sample can be easily seen.

Wallpaper Removal

One quick way to soften old wallpaper that must be scraped off is to spray it with hot water, using an ordinary tank-type garden sprayer. This throws a fine controlled mist which will wet the paper thoroughly, yet will not run down onto the floor.

Removing Plastic Wallpapers

The newer types of waterproof, stainproof wallpaper are often difficult to remove since some have a heavy plastic coating which does not allow water to penetrate so that the backing can be softened. To rectify this situation, scratch up the surface of the paper thoroughly with a sheet of very coarse sandpaper before trying to steam or soak it off.

New Paint Brushes

Before using a new, natural-bristle paint brush, it should be properly broken in if it is to give maximum service. Suspend it for twenty-four hours in raw linseed oil so that the bristles are fully covered but do not touch the bottom of the can. Then squeeze out the surplus oil, rinse in turpentine and spin dry before using.

Preparing Roller

Before starting to paint with a brand new roller cover, it is always wise to first wash the cover thoroughly with warm water and soap. Rinse well to remove any suds and to flush out all lint and dust that may have accumulated in the fiber. If an oil or alkyd-based paint is to be used, the cover should be dried thoroughly before dipping it into the paint. With water-thinned paints, the cover can be used while still damp.

Straining Paint

A quick, easy way to strain out a can of old lumpy paint is to first cut a circular piece of screen wire that just fits inside the can. Use the bottom of the can as a template and cut the screen wire about one-quarter inch less in diameter. Dropped in at the top of the can, the circular piece of wire will sink slowly to the bottom, carrying all lumps with it.

Painting Furniture

A hard-drying, exterior-type enamel is the kind of paint that should be used for both metal and wood outdoor furniture. Never use ordinary lead-and-oil house paint (some hard-drying trim paints are suitable) since house paints are comparatively soft and may chalk or rub off on your clothes.

Safe Paint Removers

Though the vast majority of chemical paint removers sold are highly inflammable and leave a waxy residue, which must be rinsed off thoroughly before the surface can be refinished, home handymen would do well to purchase only those which are neither inflammable nor waxy. Although these are usually more expensive, they completely eliminate the necessity for after-rinses or neutralizing washes. In addition, since they are also non-flammable they are much safer to use indoors where smoking or other fire hazards may be present.

Paint Removal

Steel wool wrapped around an ice pick or pencil will often remove paint from curved areas on furniture if the finish is first moistened with paint remover. If legs and rungs are lathe-turned, wrap steel wool around a piece of string and seesaw this around the turnings. A toothbrush will remove finish from the carvings.

Brush Holder

A large-headed tack or roofing nail driven into the wooden handle of the brush near the ferrule, as shown in Fig. 29, provides a convenient means of hanging the brush over the inside edge of the bucket. It serves as a brush rest between strokes, and while the bucket is being moved.

Fig. 29

APPLICATION TRICKS

Apply Evenly

Paint should never be applied in an excessively thick film, particularly when outside paint or enamel is being used. Too thick a coat will prevent proper drying underneath and will almost certainly result in wrinkling of the finish as it dries. To avoid this, brush the paint out sufficiently and apply a second coat if the first one fails to cover adequately.

Solid Foundation

Home painters should avoid applying finish coats of paint until after undercoats or primers have thoroughly hardened. Though it may seem dry in a few hours, check the label on the can for the amount of drying time recommended by the manufacturer. Applying the finish coat too soon may cause checking or wrinkling in a matter of days.

Eliminating Bubbles

To assure a bubble-free finish when applying varnish or enamel, never wipe a freshly loaded brush over the rim of the can to remove the excess. This causes a foam-like bubbling of the material, making it almost impossible to brush out smoothly. Instead, pat the sides of the bristles lightly against the inside of the can above the surface of the liquid to remove the surplus (Fig. 30). Then flow the material on liberally with moderate pressure, and cross-stroke lightly with an almost dry brush.

Fig. 30

To Avoid Skips

When painting walls or ceilings, always try to begin near the windows and work back into the darker part of the room. Reflections on the wet paint will make it easier to see if the surface is being uniformly covered. This is a particularly handy trick to remember when repainting walls or ceilings with the same color paint.

Colored Undercoats

Since most primers and undercoats are sold in white only, amateur painters often have difficulty in covering over them with the finish coat, particularly if a very dark color is being applied. To make application of this second coat easier, the homeowner should ask the dealer to sell him a few tubes of the appropriate tinting colors. These can be added to the undercoat or primer before it is applied. The color mixed need not be an exact match to the final coat. Any reasonably close shade will do the trick.

Shorty Brush

Home handymen will find it convenient to convert one of their paint brushes for use in tight corners or narrow places, and for painting between closely spaced shelves. To convert a brush for this purpose, saw off the handle so that only two or three inches is left above the ferrule. There will be enough wood left to permit grasping the brush satisfactorily, and the tool will be ideal for those tight-spot painting jobs.

Removing Skin

When partially filled cans of paint are left to stand, a skin often forms over the top. This is not particularly harmful and should in no way interfere with the rest of the paint providing the skin is cleanly removed beforehand. To do this, first use a sharp stick or a screwdriver to cut the skin away from the edge of the can around all sides. Do this job carefully so that the skin is left in one piece, if possible. The whole thing can then be lifted out neatly with two pieces of wood, used together like tongs. If any small pieces or undissolved lumps do remain, they should be strained out with cheesecloth after thorough stirring.

Using Rollers

A freshly loaded paint roller will have less tendency to cause drips or runs if the first stroke on the wall is made in an upward direction. On ceilings, make the first stroke by working away from you. Avoid spinning rapidly if you don't want to get spattered, and pick up more paint as soon as the roller cover shows signs of running dry.

Painting Wallpaper

To avoid possible trouble when painting over wallpaper, always brush out a sample of the paint on a small section of the wallpaper first. Let this dry, then check to see if coloring matter from the paper bleeds through. If this occurs, the paper should be removed before painting is resumed, or a sealer should be applied beforehand.

Wallpaper Must Be Tight

Almost any alkyd or latex-type flat wall paint can be used over wallpaper. However, make certain the paper is adhering firmly before trying to paint over it. Any slight loosening will be aggravated by the addition of a coat of paint. If the paper shows signs of pulling away, it should be removed completely before painting.

Painting Small Pieces

To speed up painting of small tables or chairs, turn them upside down on top of a workbench or sawhorse. First paint all the bottom portions which are normally hard to reach. Work from the inside to the outside, then turn the piece over and complete the upper portions.

Extension for Ceilings

The task of painting a ceiling in the average room can be speeded up by the use of a paint roller to which an extension handle is attached. Extensions of this kind are available to fit all types of roller handles so that the bulk of the job can be done without a ladder.

Painting Linoleum

Old linoleum floors can be rejuvenated by painting with two coats of porch and floor enamel after scrubbing thoroughly with a commercial wax remover. For an interesting two-toned marbelized effect, use two different colors. Apply the first color and let dry thoroughly. Then stipple the second color on with a sponge. Such a finish is very practical because it does not show scuff marks or foot tracks as much as a solid-colored floor would.

Gold Paint

All metallic gold paints eventually tarnish since they are made of bronze powders rather than of real gold. To a great extent this tarnishing can be prevented or postponed for a considerable length of time if the gold paint is given a coat of clear fresh shellac after it is dry.

Painting Radiators

Contrary to popular opinion, metallic paints (gold, silver, etc.) should never be used on radiators if maximum efficiency is to be attained. These paints tend to hold the heat in rather than allowing it to radiate outward into the room. A preferred paint to use is the same flat type as used on the walls. Flat paint not only allows more heat to escape, but when done in the same color as the walls, it also makes the unit much less noticeable. Be sure to turn radiators off and allow them to cool before painting.

Spatter-Dash Floors

To achieve a spattered finish on painted floors, first coat the floor with the background color desired and let dry thoroughly. Then dip a small brush in the contrasting color desired and strike it sharply against a stick held in the other hand. The closer to the floor the brush and stick are held, the smaller the spatters will be. Larger spatters are achieved by putting more paint on the brush and by striking across a stick held 30 to 36 inches above the floor. For maximum durability, allow spatters to dry completely, then protect with a coat of clear varnish and keep waxed.

Fast Work on Fences

To speed up the job of painting wire fences, a paint roller can be used rather than a brush. Buy one of the special, deep pile lamb's wool covers which are sold for just this purpose in most paint stores. Then roll the paint on just as you would if you were painting a wall. The deep nap will work the paint liberally into all joints as well as over the face of the wire on both sides.

Avoid Smearing

One easy way for amateur painters to avoid smearing paint onto floors or carpets while painting baseboards is to use a strip of cardboard or aluminum foil as a shield. Slide the cardboard along on the floor, following the brush as it moves along the baseboard. Any slips will cause smears on the shield rather than on the floor. When the cardboard or foil is dirty, it can be disposed of and a fresh piece substituted.

Painting Legs

To simplify the painting of small chair and table legs, drive thin nails into the bottom of each leg before starting. Standing the chair or table on these narrow supports will permit painting the leg all the way to the bottom without smearing up the floor and without worrying about sticking.

Painting Knobs

To simplify the job of painting wooden drawer knobs, tool handles and other small objects, try hanging them on a string and painting with a spray bomb. If the string is wound up and then let go, the item to be painted will spin freely. It can then be sprayed effortlessly while it turns. (See Fig. 31.)

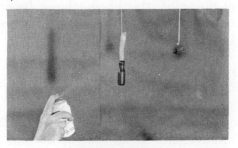

Fig. 31

Drip Catcher

To prevent open paint cans from dripping or running onto the floor and furniture, stand the can in an inexpensive paper plate. The plate will catch all drips and can be thrown away when the job is finished.

Fence Shield

To avoid a mess when spraying fences, use a piece of cardboard hooked to the top of the fence as a backboard. If there is a breeze blowing, this shield will protect plants and property on the other side from paint spray. The height of the cardboard should be the height of the fence, and it can be any width desired. Hooks can be made from metal coat hangers.

Spray Bombs

Aerosol-type paint spray bombs provide a convenient method for painting furniture and other small objects. However, trouble is sometimes encountered when paint runs or sags. This is invariably due to the fact that the user attempts to do too much with one coat. He moves the can too slowly (or not at all) in his attempt to cover completely. Instead, try moving more rapidly and applying only a thin, light coat the first time. Then double back and add a second coat if necessary. The work will go faster; there will be no runs; and less paint will actually be used.

Speed on Floors

The quickest way to paint or varnish a large floor is to use a roller rather than an ordinary paint brush. If an extension handle (available at all paint stores) is attached to the handle of the roller, the whole job can be done without bending. Simply pour a small pool of paint on the floor, then spread it around with the roller.

Emergency Lettering Brush

For lettering temporary signs when no small brushes are available, homeowners will find that cotton swabs twisted around a small stick will serve almost as well. The inexpensive swabs are available at all drug stores, and are equally handy for applying glue or other adhesives. This saves on cleaning time, since the swab is simply thrown away when the job is done.

Painting Wall Plates

Don't paint over wall switch and receptacle plates without removing them first. If the plates must be removed later, the paint will chip and leave a messy looking broken area. Remove the plates and paint the wall behind them. Then paint the plates separately and replace when dry.

Spray Booth

When spray-painting small objects with aerosol-type paint spray bombs, or with a conventional paint sprayer, a spray booth will help keep the paint where it belongs and will prevent accidental spraying of nearby floors, walls and other surfaces. An inexpensive, quickly-improvised spray booth can be made out of a large, empty carton procured from the local grocery store or from an appliance dealer. Cut off one end completely and lay the carton on its side so that the open end faces you. Objects can then be placed inside for safe, convenient spraying.

WOOD FINISHING

Cleaning Raw Wood

To clean hand prints or other dirt marks off new wood which is to receive a clear natural finish, scrub down with fine steel wool and denatured alcohol. This is not only an excellent solvent for most dirt marks, it also acts as a very mild bleach on the raw wood. Work in a well-ventilated room and do not smoke as denatured alcohol is highly flammable.

Filler Is Needed

Regardless of whether they are to be finished with opaque paint or clear varnish, open-grained woods such as oak or mahogany require a filler if a perfectly smooth finish is to be achieved. The filler comes in paste form and is thinned to brushing consistency with turpentine. It should be applied according to the directions on the can, and is available in many paint stores in assorted colors.

Removing Dust

Sanding is an important first step in achieving a smooth finish. However, its effect will be completely nullified if all resulting dust is not carefully removed before finish coats are applied. Special tacky rags, available at paint stores, are best for this job. A soft-bristled brush or a vacuum cleaner also works well. Dry rags should be avoided since most will leave undesirable lint.

Varnishing

Varnish will flow out more smoothly when it is slightly warm. If work must be done outdoors in chilly weather, or in an unheated garage or basement, try heating the varnish slightly beforehand. To do this, stand the varnish can in a second, larger can filled with hot water. Keep warm by placing on a hot plate or by replacing with freshly heated water as the original water cools.

Thinning Shellac

Most shellac is usually sold in five pound "cut" or strength. For practically all work the shellac should be thinned with denatured alcohol, usually about one-half on the first coat and one-third on the second.

Storing Shellac

Unlike most paints, shellac will not keep for very long and should only be used when relatively fresh. Its life can be prolonged to some extent by storing in glass jars rather than in cans. Even so, shellac which is much more than six months old should be discarded.

Satin Finish

When finishing furniture with varnish or enamel, the home painter would do well to use a semi-gloss varnish or enamel rather than a high-gloss finish. The semi-gloss finish has a pleasant, satiny look which simulates hand-rubbed furniture, and it is less likely to show brush marks or other defects when dry. In most cases these finishes are just as durable and washable as the high-gloss finishes, particularly for interior use.

Applying Stain

A handy way to apply oil stains or water stains on raw wood is to use a cellulose sponge instead of a brush. A sponge will require less frequent dipping, and will make it easier to regulate the amount being applied. In addition, the square edges help when working in corners or along edges.

For a Smooth Finish

Never shake or stir clear glossy varnish before using it. Agitation of this kind will only whip small air bubbles into the material and will make it difficult to brush out. The bubbles remain in the dried varnish film and will make it impossible to achieve a truly smooth finish.

Hand-Rubbed Effect

To achieve a hand-rubbed effect on a newly varnished high gloss surface, let the varnish harden for three or four days. Use a pad of No. 0000 steel wool to rub on a thin layer of good quality paste wax. Rub on lightly in parallel strokes, working with the grain. The result will be a smooth, satiny finish which can be buffed to a lustrous sheen after the wax dries.

Save Remover

When paint remover must be used on chair or table legs, a great deal is often wasted because it runs rapidly down the leg if too much is applied. To permit applying as heavily as desired without waste, stand each leg in an old coffee can before beginning (Fig. 32). The surplus which runs down can then be salvaged by pouring back into the original container when the job is done.

Fig. 32

Burning Designs

To burn initials, monograms, and other intricate designs into wood, here is an easy method. Simply paint on the design you want with a fine brush, using ordinary fingernail polish. Light one end of the polish with a match and the flame will neatly follow the design, charring the wood along the painted path.

Imitation Inlay

To create an interesting, decorative effect when finishing natural wood with a stained finish, here is a method which simulates an inlay made of a lighter wood. Outline the design desired by scribing with the point of a sharp knife, then paint the area inside this design with a thin coat of clear, fresh shellac. Allow to dry, then stain the entire piece as usual. The area that has been shellacked will not absorb the stain and will stay light when wiped off, thus providing an attractive contrast in color.

CLEAN-UP AND STORAGE

For a Tight Seal

The rim around most paint cans usually becomes caked with paint and makes it difficult to replace the lid properly. This not only wastes paint, it permits the remainder to dry up in the can. Eliminate this by using a hammer and a nail set to punch small holes in the bottom of the groove around the rim before you start to paint (Fig. 33). This will permit trapped paint to drip back into the can where it belongs.

Fig. 33

Color Record

To simplify future color matching and to have a record of each paint color that is used around the house, the wise homeowner will coat a stiff piece of cardboard with a sample of the paint as it is being applied to the house. This card can be filed for future reference when color samples are needed while shopping for accessories, or for matching. It will keep better than a liquid sample since there is no danger of drying out or jelling.

Cleaning Paint Pots

To clean out pails or roller pans after a paint job is finished, sprinkle in enough sand to cover all the wet paint on the inside. Then scrub out with old newspapers, rubbing the sand around much as you would a scouring powder. Instead of sand you can use sawdust if it is more readily available.

Cleaning Paint Tray

To eliminate the job of cleaning out a paint tray after using a roller, try lining the tray beforehand with ordinary brown wrapping paper. Tuck it snugly into all corners and then pour the paint in over the paper. When clean-up time rolls around, simply strip out the paper lining. All that will be left in the tray is a slight amount of oil without pigment. This can be wiped out with a dry rag. If preferred, aluminum foil can also be used.

Prevent Paint Splatter

When replacing the cover on a partly used can of paint, spread a rag over the lid before hammering it shut or before stepping on it to seal it. Excess paint that has accumulated in the rim will be caught by the rag instead of being splattered onto clothes or hands, or instead of oozing down over the sides of the can.

Cleaning Hands

To simplify the job of cleaning hands after painting, or after working with greasy tools, rub some protective cream onto the skin before starting. Special material is sold in most paint and hardware stores and enables all grime to be easily washed away with ordinary soap and water when the day's work is done.

Identifying Paint

To identify the color of the paint in a closed can, always dab a liberal smear on the outside before sealing it. This will not only tell you the color of the paint, it will also provide you with an accurate color swatch which can be matched years later should the original paint spoil.

Storing Paint

To prevent a partly empty can of paint from skinning up excessively, try this simple trick. Before closing the cover pour a few drops of turpentine gently over the surface. Let it run down the side of a stick so that it floats on top. Seal tightly and then put the can away without shaking or tipping it. Another trick that works well is to close the can tightly and put in on a shelf upside down. The paint itself will form an airtight seal over the lid, preventing it from drying out. If any skin does form, it will be out of the way at the bottom when the can is turned right-side-up again before opening.

Brush Care

After brushes have been thoroughly cleaned, they should be tightly wrapped in heavy aluminum foil or brown wrapping paper before storing. Failure to do so will often cause brushes to lose their shape, since bristles may become curled or mangled and will acquire a permanent set which will be difficult to work out later on. Comb before wrapping, and store by laying it flat on a shelf.

Cleaning Rollers

Before washing out the cover on a freshly used paint roller, always roll out as much of the excess paint as possible so that washing will be easier. The best way to do this is to use a stack of old newspapers. Roll the paint-filled cover on the top sheet of newspaper till it becomes saturated. Then tear off and roll again on the next sheet. Repeat this process until no more paint comes out, then wash. For best results take off the cover completely while washing so that the solvent can act inside the core to prevent dried paint from hardening on the inside.

Paint Funnel

When paint must be poured from a large container into a small jar for storage, a handy disposable funnel can be improvised from an inexpensive cone-shaped paper cup. Snip off the bottom end with a pair of scissors and use the remainder as a funnel. The cup can be thrown away when the job is done, thus eliminating another clean-up.

5

Plumbing, Heating and Electrical Work

PLUMBING REPAIRS

Mark Valves

When water, gas or other valves must be shut off quickly because of an emergency, confusion sometimes occurs because the homeowner is uncertain as to just which valve controls what. To eliminate this possibility, take time out to hang identifying tags on all shut-off valves throughout the house. For best results use different colored tags for water, gas, steam, etc.

Washer Sizes

When the home handyman prepares to change a washer in a leaky faucet, he often does so on a weekend holiday, or in the evening when all stores are closed. Then when the faucet is disassembled, he finds that among the assortment on hand he is missing the one size needed for that particular faucet. To prevent this happening in the future, make a note of the size washers needed for each faucet, and mark this information with crayon on the bottom of the sink or appliance so that your supply can be replenished before the faucet is taken apart.

Identifying Pipelines

To help speed up the identification of household shut-off valves and pipelines when repairs or alterations are made, mark all pipes in the basement with identifying dabs of colored paint. Use one color for all hot water lines, another color for cold water pipes, and additional colors for gas lines, waste pipes and the like. You can also color-code them in the same way to tell which room each pipe supplies.

Clogged Drains

When household drains in bathrooms or kitchens become clogged, handymen usually rely on a "plumber's friend" or "plunger" (a rubber suction cup on the end of a handle) to relieve the situation. To use the plunger most effectively, you should remember that the clearing action occurs on the upstroke rather than on the downstroke, so after pressing downward, pull up vigorously for maximum suction action. The cup works by drawing the obstruction back up into the pipe so that it can be broken up by the downrushing water. Forcing it downward may only pack the debris in more tightly and thus makes it harder to break up.

Frozen Drains

When summer cottages are vacated for the winter, or when homes are left without heat for a great length of time, homeowners usually remember to shut off water and to drain all pipes as protection against freezing. However, drain traps in each fixture are often forgotten. To prevent water in drains from freezing and possibly bursting the pipes, a pint of kerosene or automobile antifreeze should be poured down each trap, including the toilets, before the house is vacated.

Prevent Pipes Freezing

When water pipes pass through unheated garages, crawl spaces or attics, they may sometimes freeze during extremely cold periods, especially if a particular pipe feeds a circuit that is seldom used. To prevent this, thermostatically controlled heating cables can be purchased. These are wrapped around the pipe when winter sets in and are then left plugged in continuously until all danger of a freeze-up is passed. The cables are available at most electrical supply and hardware stores, and come in various lengths and wattages.

Hammering Pipes

When water pipes hammer or chatter every time a faucet is turned on, the trouble is frequently due to a pipe which is improperly supported at some point along its length. Check the lengths of pipe wherever they are exposed in the basement to see that all mounting straps are tight (Fig. 34). The pipe should be solidly anchored at frequent in-

Fig. 34

tervals along its length. Watch for places where the pipe has give or where it has sagged out of line so that vibrations are set up when water rushes rapidly through it.

Gurgling Pipes

The homeowner who has a two-story house with bathrooms one above the other will sometimes be troubled by a gurgling noise in the downstairs washbowl whenever the upstairs basin is drained. In extreme cases there may even be some backup of waste water from above in the downstairs bowl. Usually this trouble is caused by a partially clogged air vent stack (this is the large vent pipe which sticks up above the roof). It may be that wasps or birds have built nests near the top, or a back-flow of suds may have caused partial stoppage in the vent. To correct this, push a stiff wire or "plumber's snake" down through the vent stack from up on the roof. Once the vent has been cleared, air will be able to escape freely and waste water will flow out quietly.

Wire "Snake"

When a toilet drain is clogged, a makeshift tool for freeing it is sometimes almost as effective as many professional tools. In an emergency a piece of coat hanger wire can be bent into the shape of a bobby pin, but with the last half inch or so of the ends crossed. This can then be pushed down the drain, crossed ends first, and twisted. The wire ends will pick up matted hair, bits of paper, and other stubborn clogging debris.

Running Toilet

When toilet tanks keep running constantly after the toilet is flushed, the trouble may be due to a faulty float-ball inside the tank. To check this, lift up on the end of the metal or plastic float-ball slightly to see if it shuts off the water and stops the hissing sound after the tank is full. If it does, then chances are that the float-ball is leaking and waterlogged, hence it is not shutting off the intake valve as it should. Unscrew the ball and shake it vigorously. If you can hear water rattling around inside, it is leaking and should be replaced with a new one. If it is not leaking, it may be that the rod needs to be bent downward slightly so that the float will apply a little additional upward pressure on the intake valve shut-off mechanism.

Persistent Drips

If a faucet starts to drip again soon after a new washer has been inserted, chances are that more than just another washer replacement is needed. The seat against which the washer presses may have become damaged and needs regrinding or replacing. Special kits and tools for this purpose are available at hardware stores and plumbing supply houses.

Noisy Faucets

A normally quiet faucet that howls or chatters every time it is turned on is frequently easy to remedy by simply putting in a new washer. To play safe replace the brass screw that holds it in place at the same time, then tighten securely.

Air Cushion

When water rushing through a pipe is suddenly slammed to a stop by a quickly closed valve, a hammering noise sometimes results. A cure for this can often be effected by installation of an air chamber or air hammer above the

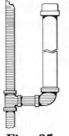

Fig. 35

highest faucet in the house. This attachment is spliced into the pipe with an ordinary tee-fitting wherever the pipe is exposed (Fig. 35). It consists of a two- or three-foot vertical length of pipe which is tightly capped at the upper end. If all upstairs pipes are enclosed, the next best location for the air chamber is right next to the water meter.

To Loosen Joints

Threaded pipe joints which have been frozen tight by heavy accumulations of rust can usually be loosened with normal wrench pressure if a few drops of household ammonia are first applied around the joint. Give the ammonia a few minutes to work and help it to penetrate by tapping lightly with a hammer to set up a slight vibration.

Recessed Faucets

When washers must be changed on shower or bathtub faucets which are recessed into the wall, difficulty will often be encountered in getting at the large nut that holds the spindle in place. This nut is often below the surface of the tile so that it can't be reached with an ordinary wrench. If the special tool that plumbers use is unavailable, try an inexpensive spark plug wrench. This has a deep socket and will often do the trick nicely.

Protect Chrome

When using a pipe wrench or pliers on chrome-plated plumbing fixtures, extra care is required to protect the polished metal against scratching. The easiest way to do this is to first wrap the pipe or fitting with electrician's tape or with ordinary adhesive tape. This provides a non-slip surface which prevents damage to the chrome.

Polishing Fixtures

To polish old faucets or other plumbing fixtures which appear hopelessly corroded and pitted, try using automobile rubbing compound scrubbed on vigorously with a damp rag. A heavy string coated with the abrasive material can be drawn back and forth around narrow curves or in tight corners.

Sweat-Soldering

When sweat-soldering joints on copper pipe with a propane torch, joints which are close together sometimes loosen up from the nearby heat. To prevent this, wrap each joint with a wet rag as it is completed. This will keep it from absorbing enough heat to re-melt the solder when the flame is applied to an adjoining member. If the cloth dries out, dampen it again.

Measuring Pipe

To measure the outside diameter of a piece of pipe (or other small round object) so that an accurate replacement can be purchased, an ordinary monkey wrench can be used. Tighten the wrench lightly onto the outside of the pipe and then slide it off without disturbing the setting. Measure the distance between the jaws to get the outside diameter.

Sealing Pipe Joints

When no pipe joint compound is available to seal threaded joints in galvanized or black iron pipe, white lead paint or exterior house paint can be used instead. Smear the heavy-bodied liquid liberally onto the male threads immediately before tightening.

HEATING AND COOLING

Thermostat Location

When a thermostat controls the heat in the entire house, it is important that it be located where it will give a true reading of the average temperature throughout the house. If it is located where it is frequently in the path of cold drafts from open doors or windows, it will call for more heat than needed and will keep most rooms in the house overheated. If it is located near a lamp, television set, or other source of heat, it will read warmer than it should and will not send up enough heat.

Venting Radiators

All radiators in hot water heating systems have little air vents located in one end at the top. These vents let out trapped air so that hot water can enter and circulate freely. Some vents do this automatically, but others must be bled manually. If yours are not automatic, use the special key provided, or a screwdriver, to bleed them at the beginning of each heating season. Open each valve till water runs out, then close immediately. (See Fig. 36.)

Fig. 36

Drafts From Behind

Sometimes thermostats do not work properly because drafts from inside the hollow wall come out through the opening through which the wires are drawn. This cold air comes into the back of the thermostat and causes the elements to switch on the furnace even though the room is warm enough. To prevent this, unscrew the thermostat from the wall and plug the opening behind it with a small wad of caulking compound or with fireproof insulation.

More Heat

To get more heat out of your radiators, try slipping a sheet of aluminum foil behind each one when the heating season begins. To keep it in place, tape the foil to the wall or staple it onto a sheet of heavy cardboard or thin hardboard.

Two Controls

Most homeowners who have a hot water heating system know that the temperature of the house can be controlled by operating the thermostat located somewhere in the living quarters of the house. However, many do not realize that there is another control downstairs that should also be adjusted seasonally. Usually called the aquastat, this control regulates the temperature of the water in the system. In the winter, when the entire house is drawing heat from the boiler, this aquastat should be set higher to assure hot water in the bathrooms and kitchens as well as in the heating system. In the summer fuel economies can be realized by turning the aquastat down fifteen or twenty degrees since hot water is needed only at the faucets and not in the main boiler or radiators. The exact temperature setting will vary with make or brand of boiler and can best be determined by consulting the manufacturer or heating serviceman.

Faster Heat

When a steam radiator fails to heat up fast enough, or when it doesn't get hot all the way across, the trouble is most likely due to a sticky vent valve. This little valve is located at one end near the top and is supposed to let air escape so steam can enter. Sticky valves can sometimes be cleaned, but in most cases a new one is advisable. Get one of the adjustable kind so that you can control the time it takes to heat up whenever necessary (Fig. 37). These will permit adjustment so that one or more rooms can be heated up faster than the others.

Fig. 37

For a Cooler House

Concrete patios and other large paved areas adjoining the house can reflect a great deal of heat into the house during the summer when the sun shines directly on them. Cut down on the amount of heat reflected, and also make sitting on the patio a bit more comfortable, by hosing the cement down several times a day during hot spells.

Keep Heat Out

Homes can be kept cooler on hot summer days if the shades are not raised on the sunny side of the house, and if windows are not thrown wide open in the morning. Keeping shades down and windows closed on the sunny walls will help keep the midday heat outside, and will help keep the cooler night air trapped inside the house. Raise shades and open windows when the sun starts to set in the evening and the air becomes cooler.

Air Conditioner Efficiency

Room air conditioners will operate better and with less wasted power if homeowners will remember to follow the manufacturer's instruction manual more closely. For example, failure to change the air filter (or to clean it) when it is dirty will cut down greatly on the unit's output, and may overload it dangerously. Also, remember to clean the outside grilles and to lubricate if required.

ELECTRICAL REPAIRS

Blowing Fuses

Most household lighting circuits are fused with 15-ampere fuses, which means they are designed to carry no more than about 1400 watts. By plugging in too many appliances on the same circuit, and by overloading individual outlets with multiple plugs, circuits can sometimes be overloaded so that fuses blow even though no shorts or other defects occur. To prevent this, you should avoid plugging in too many high-wattage appliances at one time. You should also have extra circuits added by a competent electrical contractor if frequent fuse blowing occurs on some circuits.

Emergency Kit

Since minor electrical repairs often have to be made in a hurry when fuses blow and lights suddenly go out, homeowners should put together an emergency kit with all needed materials readily available in one place. As an example, the kit should contain: extra fuses in various sizes, a small flashlight, insulating tape, screwdriver, pliers and a handy test light.

Splicing Wire

When making a splice in a two-conductor wire, always cut each wire so that the ends of the wires are uneven by an equal amount. In other words, cut each wire so that one leg is an inch longer than the other. Then join them with the two splices offset so that the bare part on one wire is

Fig. 38

next to the insulated part of another wire (Fig. 38). Twist each splice tightly together, then wrap with plastic insulating tape. The result will be two neat, separated joints with no danger of bare wires contacting each other, and with no bulky mass of tape occurring in one spot.

Soldered Joint

When electric wires are to be joined together so as to form a permanent splice, experts all agree that soldered joints are safest and will last the longest. However, the wires should be twisted tightly together beforehand so that a firm mechanical bond is assured before solder is applied. The solder should not be depended upon for strength; it merely insures good metal-to-metal contact and prevents eventual loosening due to vibration or other movement of the wire.

Terminal Screws

When twisting electrical wires around terminal screws on plugs or other appliances, always twist the wire around the screw in a clockwise direction. Then when the screw is tightened, the wire will not be as likely to unwind or untwist. Instead, it will get wound up even tighter as the terminal screw is tightened.

Protect Cords

Rubber-covered electrical cords can be protected against premature drying out and cracking by rubbing on a thin coat of wax or paraffin at periodic intervals. Wipe on with one cloth and then draw through a second dry cloth several minutes later to remove excess and prevent stickiness.

Using Extension Cords

To keep extension cords from pulling apart when portable tools or appliances are plugged into them, first loop the ends together by tying a loose knot with cords as shown in Fig. 39. Joined in this manner, the cords cannot accidentally be pulled apart no matter how much one end is tugged.

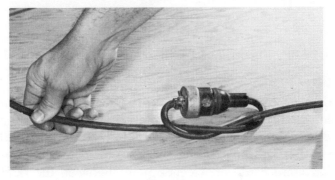

Fig. 39

Storing Extension Cords

To keep long extension cords from knotting up or kinking badly when storing them, try wrapping the cord around an empty tin can such as a large juice can before putting it way. Tuck the last turn under itself to keep the cord from unraveling.

Electrician's Tape

When making electrical repairs around the house, a length of friction tape can be kept always handy by rolling up a miniature spool on the screwdriver blade. Wind several feet around the blade near the top where it enters the handle. Short lengths can then be torn off as needed without the necessity of hunting for a spool of the tape each time.

Safer Connection

When connecting stranded wires to an electrical plug, always twist the individual fine strands tightly together before fastening them under the screwhead. Then, for maximum safety, solder these ends lightly to form a solid mass (Fig. 40). This will permanently prevent fraying and eliminates the possibility of loose strands causing a short.

Fig. 40

Tight Plugs

Many electrical plugs have prongs made of strips of metal which are bent over to form a double thickness. When plugs of this type lose their springiness they do not fit tightly in the outlets and poor contact results. To correct this, insert a thin knife blade or ice pick point between the doubled-over leaves of metal and spread them apart slightly. This increases tension on the prongs when they are inserted.

Tape Dispenser

A discarded cellulose tape dispenser is handy for use with electrician's friction tape or plastic tape. It not only serves as a handy holder and storage container for the tape, but the serrated edge also simplifies the job of tearing off the exact length needed.

Rusty Bulb Sockets

Light bulbs on outdoor porches and other exposed areas sometimes corrode at the base and tend to "freeze" in the socket. To prevent this, smear a very thin layer of grease or petroleum jelly over the metal threads of a new bulb before inserting it in an outdoor socket.

APPLIANCE CARE

Save Literature

When a new home appliance or power tool is delivered, always make certain you read all instruction booklets and other accompanying literature carefully before putting the gadget to work for the first time. Fill out and mail whatever guarantee cards accompany the item, and, most important of all, be sure you file this literature in a safe place where it can be referred to later on whenever repairs or spare parts are needed. The booklet may tell you how to make some of the simpler repairs and adjustments yourself, and will give you serial numbers, model numbers and other pertinent data which you may need in the future when trouble occurs.

Lubrication

When oiling small motors and other delicate moving parts of appliances, most manufacturers recommend that only a few drops of light oil be applied. To simplify the task of measuring out the required amount, and to avoid dangerous over-oiling, apply the oil with an eyedropper so that the exact amount can be accurately measured.

Clean Motors

Electric motors in appliances and workshop machines can have their efficiency cut considerably if heavy accumulations of dust or grit are allowed to accumulate on the inside around the windings, bearings or commutator. To prevent trouble before it happens, the homeowner should get in the habit of cleaning all motors thoroughly with a vacuum cleaner at least twice a year. Use the narrow crevice attachment to suck out dust and dirt where possible. Then use the blowing end to puff out the remainder. Needless to say, make certain the motor being cleaned is turned off before starting this job.

Preventing Motor Burn-Out

If a homeowner has trouble with motors on power tools or appliances burning out for no apparent reason—especially if several are plugged in on the same circuit—he should call in a competent electrical contractor to check his wiring and to check the loads on each circuit. When circuits are overloaded, voltages delivered at the outlets will drop. Though this may not be severe enough to blow a fuse, if continued long enough it may eventually cause motors to burn out. The only sure cure lies in adding extra circuits, or in having a larger meter and fuse box installed.

Prevent Kinking

To prevent electric power cords on portable appliances from twisting and kinking, home handymen can cover them with a spiral plastic cord wrapper of the type that is sold in many hardware and home-furnishing stores for use on telephone cords. These are installed by simply twisting in place around the outside of the cord.

Electric Plugs

To keep plastic electric plugs on appliances from cracking when they are accidentally banged or crushed, wrap them with one or two layers of plastic or rubber tape, particularly if the appliance is to be used around the garage or workshop. This method can also be used to make an emergency repair on one of these plugs after the damage has been done. However, replace it with a new plug as soon as possible.

Parts Tray

When making repairs on small appliances, screws, gears and other miniature parts are often easily misplaced. Eliminate this problem by folding up a small tray of white cardboard or aluminum foil. The light-colored material will make parts easier to spot, and the lip that is folded around the edge will prevent the parts from accidentally rolling away.

Replacing Lamp Cords

When the electrical cords on floor lamps become frayed or cracked, the safest procedure lies in replacing the cord entirely rather than in merely splicing on a new piece where the frayed part shows. To work the new cord up through the base and column of the lamp, remove the socket at the top and disconnect the old cord first. Tie a long piece of string onto the end of this cord before pulling it out through the bottom. Then after the old cord has been removed, the string can be used to draw the new lamp cord through from the top. Tie the new cord onto the top end of the string and pull through. Then attach the wire to the socket and replace at the top of the lamp.

Doorbell Repair

If a doorbell or chime fails to ring when the button outside is pushed, chances are that the trouble is in the button itself. To check this, remove it from its mounting and short the two wires in back by touching a screwdriver across the terminals (Fig. 41). If this causes the bell to ring, then the button is

Fig. 41

at fault and a new one should be purchased and installed. If this is not the trouble, then check the transformer downstairs near the fuse box, and check the connections at the bell or chime itself.

Appliance Touch-Up

When the finish on a kitchen appliance becomes scratched or nicked so that the bare metal underneath is exposed, it should be touched up as quickly as possible to prevent rusting. Special touch-up materials are sold in most paint, hardware and appliance stores, or you can use any good grade of enamel in a matching color. In an emergency even a little clear fingernail polish could be used to protect the metal till a permanent repair can be made. Apply the touch-up with a small cotton swab wrapped around a toothpick, and build up in layers if necessary to fill in a deep scratch.

6

Miscellaneous Housekeeping Hints

ASSORTED TIMESAVERS

Light for Emergencies

To prevent accidents and confusion when storms knock down power lines, it is wise to prepare for storm damage ahead of time by keeping emergency lights on hand. Locate a few miniature, inexpensive pocket flashlights in strategic spots around the home. Keep one near the fuse box, one near the cellar stairs, one near the furnace, and one near any other potential danger area.

When Lights Go Out

Simplify the job of locating flashlights, tools and other items when lights suddenly go out during a power failure by taking time now to paint on dabs of luminous paint, or to stick on strips of luminous tape. These will glow in the dark and make the emergency supplies much easier to locate.

Protect Hardware

Brass doorknobs, escutcheon plates and other ornamental hardware can be protected from corrosion and pitting by periodically rubbing on a thin layer of paste wax. Clean thoroughly with metal polish or scouring powder first, then rub on the wax and buff vigorously when dry. Renew once or twice a year to assure continuing protection.

Protecting Candles

Tall decorative candles often lose shape or wilt during very hot weather—or when set up on candlesticks in over-heated rooms. To prevent this happening, dip the entire candle in thinned shellac (about three-pound cut) and then hang it up by the wick to dry. The shellac will stiffen the candle and protect it against wilting, but will in no way interfere with its burning properly.

Protect Walls

To keep the corners of picture frames from scratching painted or papered walls against which they are hung, try pushing a thumb tack into the back of the two lower corners. The smooth heads will slide easily, leaving no marks on the wall when the picture is shifted for dusting.

Touch-Up Paint

When small chips or scratches on painted walls or wood-work must be touched up and no leftover paint is available, a small quantity of the needed color can usually be mixed by using a few drops of the children's poster paints. Inter-mixing the primary shades will give almost any tint desired, and the easily mixed water paint can then be dabbed on with a pointed brush. The touch-up will not be washable, but it will serve nicely as a temporary repair until the next coat of paint is applied. It can be made washable by coating with thin shellac or varnish.

Prevent Lids Sticking

To eliminate the annoying problem of screw top lids and corks sticking on jars or cans which contain glue, shellac, or other adhesives, here is a simple solution. The first time the lid is removed rub a small amount of petroleum jelly over the inside of the threads on the lid. Renewed occasionally, this will keep lids from sticking in the future.

Lengthen Broom Life

Ordinary brooms wear down rapidly when used to sweep up rough cement floors in basements or garages. Their lives can be lengthened considerably by dipping the ends of the bristles into a shallow pan of thinned shellac.

Pouring Trick

To simplify the job of pouring a fine stream of liquid from a bottle or can, hold a large nail or pointed lead pencil across the opening before pouring. If done gradually, the liquid will flow down along the sides of the pencil or nail and will stream evenly off the point into the exact location desired. (See Fig. 42.)

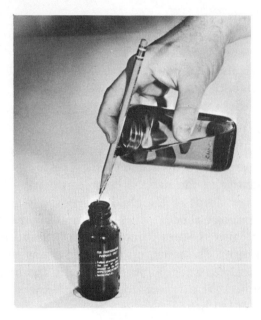

Fig. 42

Tighten Handles

When the threaded wooden handle on a floor brush or other tool works loose, emergency repairs can be quickly made by unscrewing the handle and then wrapping the exposed threads with several layers of cellophane tape. Twisting the handle back into its socket will squeeze the tape into the threads and will take up the slack nicely.

Fire Safety

Be sure all volatile and inflammable liquids such as solvents, torch fuels, gasoline, etc., are stored in metal cans with non-leaking tops. Such liquids stored in glass bottles may expand from heat and burst the container. If this happens with a spark or open flame nearby, you may end up with a serious fire.

Wax on Woodwork

When waxing painted woodwork, remember that the wax will have to be removed completely before the trim can be repainted. For this reason, use the liquid self-polishing kind. It can be easily removed when necessary with warm, soapy water and will not require the use of strong solvents.

Kitchen Ventilator

A kitchen ventilating fan is practically a must during the summertime to exhaust hot air and obnoxious odors. However, installation of a conventional wall-type unit is often too difficult for the home handyman to tackle—or the kitchen may be in a rented apartment or house so that cutting of an opening in the outside wall is impractical. One simple way to solve this problem is to install a small exhaust fan in the upper half of a double-hung window which is near the stove. Cut a sheet of plywood for a snug fit inside the window frame, then cut a hole in the center of the plywood to accommodate the fan. Mounted in this way, the fan can be taken down and stored during cold weather or when not in use, and can be quickly replaced when needed without use of tools.

Prevent Sliding

Kitchen step stools and tables with metal legs can be prevented from sliding or slipping on waxed floors if rubber crutch tips are slid over the bottom of each leg. These come in various sizes and are sold by most drug stores and all surgical supply houses.

Emergency Glides

When heavy crates or large pieces of furniture must be slid along cellar floors, garage floors, or driveways, corrugated metal caps from soda bottles make handy temporary glides which will greatly simplify the job. Put one cap upside down under each corner and tap with a hammer so the metal edge digs in. The corrugations will hold the cap in place, and the smooth top will then permit sliding easily.

Jar Opener

An ordinary squeeze-type nutcracker makes an excellent "wrench" for opening tight-fitting caps on small-mouthed jars or cans (Fig. 43). Apply only moderate pressure—just

Fig. 43

enough to keep it from slipping. On cans be careful you do not squeeze so hard that the top is bent out of shape.

Hose Washers

Rubber washers for hose couplings have a way of frequently getting misplaced just when they are most needed. To keep them always handy so that they can be instantly located when needed, slip them over a large nail driven into the wall near where the hose is stored. Drive the nail at a slight downward angle so that washers will not slide off.

Mixing Containers

Finding suitable containers in which to mix small amounts of glue, paint, or other materials is difficult—and often expensive if the material ruins the container. By bending up four sides of a small piece of aluminum foil, however, one gets a small leakproof tray of any size. It does the job, then is thrown away.

Cutting Foam Rubber

This versatile material is awkward to cut neatly with an ordinary knife or scissors. However, if compressed tightly beforehand by pressing down on it with a flat board, it will slice easily with a long-bladed sharp knife, or on a paper trimming board. Dip the blade in water to lubricate it if it tends to "grab."

Handy Sticks

Wooden tongue depressors of the kind used by physicians are handy to keep around the home and workshop. They make convenient, disposable applicators for all types of glue, mastic and adhesive, and are also handy as mixing sticks or paddles when stirring small cans of paint or similar material. The depressors are comparatively inexpensive and are available at most drug stores.

Improvised Level

When the householder needs a temporary surface level to make certain that a piece of furniture or a large appliance is standing level, a quick one can be improvised from an ordinary glass measuring cup which has markings on both sides. If the cup is filled with water to any one of the marks, it will show that the surface is level when the water contacts the marks on all sides of the cup.

Cutting Out Pages

To cut pages cleanly out of a magazine or book, a sharp knife or razor blade is ordinarily used. However, unless extreme care is used the razor blade will usually cut through pages below, removing sheets that you did not want to damage. To prevent this, slide a sheet of stiff cardboard under the page before slicing. This will provide a firm backing which assures a neat cut and will prevent damage to other pages.

Protect Blades

Single-edged razor blades are used around many homes for clipping articles out of magazines and newspapers and for other cutting jobs where a very sharp blade is required. Since only the corner of the blade is used, protection against accidental cuts can be provided by covering most of the edge with a strip of tape. When the exposed end dulls, the tape can be moved over to expose the other end while covering up the original end.

Preserving Brick

Real brick has become increasingly popular for use on indoor walls in modern homes. To help keep them clean and to prevent stains from soaking in, apply a thin coat of clear penetrating wood sealer, mixed half-and-half with turpentine. Make certain the bricks are clean and dry first.

Rope Knots

To prevent knots on the ends of venetian blind cords and sash cords from untying or unraveling, dip them in shellac while they are still tight. Let the knot soak up all the shellac the rope will absorb, then allow it to dry for about half an hour before using.

Emergency Funnel

When liquids or powders must be poured from large containers into a narrow-necked jar or can, a funnel of the right size is seldom at hand. The problem can be quickly solved with ordinary kitchen-type aluminum foil. Fold double to give added strength, then roll into a cone to create a shape which will serve as an effective funnel. The small end of the cone can be rolled as tight as needed to fit into the neck of the bottle. (See Fig. 44.)

Fig. 44

Lengthy Matches

On those occasions when the housewife finds it necessary to light tall, hard-to-reach candles, or a deep fire in the fireplace, ordinary short matchsticks make it necessary for her to stretch or climb needlessly. In addition, she may have to bring her hand dangerously close to the fire. To simplify this job, use an ordinary drinking straw. Light the end of this first, then use it as a colorful taper for lighting the candles or the fire.

Large Blackboard

Parents interested in providing large blackboards for the youngsters can create one out of any smooth sheet of hardboard or on any large flat wall surface. Simply paint with two coats of flat black enamel (available at all paint stores) or ask for special blackboard paints which are also available. These paints can be put on over any paintable surface after a suitable primer has been applied.

Household Clamp

For small gluing jobs around the home when no conventional carpenter's clamp is available, pressure can often be applied with an ordinary spring-grip pants hanger. Strips of wax paper can be used to protect the face of the hanger against adhesive which may ooze out.

Metal Legs

A length of ordinary pipe threaded at one end and a standard pipe flange can be used to improvise inexpensive metal legs for work tables or picnic tables. Screw the flange to the underside of the table top, then twist the threaded end of the pipe into the flange. To protect finished floors, rubber crutch tips can be slipped over the bottom end of the pipe.

Holiday Hint

To hang holiday wreaths and other decorations during the Christmas season without damaging doors or walls, use paste-up picture hangers which are sold in all art supply stores. The swivel hook is mounted on a strong, adhesive-coated tape. When this is moistened it will stick firmly onto any smooth wall or door and will support up to fifteen pounds in weight. Sold as a package of six for less than a quarter, these picture hangers can be easily removed without damage to the surface by soaking with water.

Removing Dents

The best way to hammer out dents from pots, pans, or other objects made of sheet metal is to first lay the dented object over a box of sand. Then hammer from the inside with a rubber mallet, or use a hammer with a rubber crutch tip slipped over the head. The sand gives solid support so that no new dents are created, yet it permits the metal to give under the hammer blows.

Removing Decals

The easiest way to remove a decal without damaging the finish underneath is to cover it with a wet washcloth and then press a hot iron over the cloth. Within a few minutes the steam will soften up the old decal to permit easy removal.

Storing Small Parts

Plastic ice cube trays make excellent miniature storage drawers for small tacks, nuts, bolts and other miscellaneous hardware. They also serve as handy sorting trays for temporary storage of tiny parts when working on small, complicated models.

Storing Washers

Washers and nuts are always difficult to find in the average home handyman's scrap drawer One easy way to keep them handy is to slip them over the open end of a safety pin or diaper pin. Assorted washers and nuts can then be kept always visible and together by closing the pin and hanging it over a nail in an exposed location.

CLEANING AND STAIN REMOVAL

Cleaning Blinds

A pair of mitts made out of old turkish towels can speed the job of cleaning venetian blinds. To make these, outline your hand on a sheet of paper, then use this as a template to cut the toweling about an inch larger all the way around. Sew together, then turn inside out. With one of these both sides of each slat can be wiped at the same time.

Protect Sills

To keep window sills from water spotting when rainstorms occur while the windows are open, rub on a thin coat of good quality paste wax. This coating will protect the painted woodwork, and will make it easy to wipe off moisture without staining. Remember to remove the wax before repainting.

Cleaning Windows

To save climbing and lugging of ladders when outside windows must be cleaned, try using a long hose brush of the type that screws onto the end of a garden hose. Usually sold for scrubbing cars, these brushes have hollow handles through which the water flows. Models are available with shut-off valves built in and with detergent dispensers in the handle.

Picture Frame Marks

When pictures that have been hanging for some time are removed, a dark or discolored area is frequently left on the wall behind them. This is usually caused by lack of circulation so that dust accumulates to darken the wall covering. To prevent this, drive two large carpet tacks or rubber-headed bumper tacks in the lower corners of each picture frame before hanging it (Fig. 45). This will hold the picture away from the wall and will permit air to circulate behind it.

Fig. 45

Wallpaper Stains

If promptly tackled, many grease stains can be removed from wallpaper with a sheet of clean white blotting paper and an ordinary electric iron. Lay the blotting paper over the stain and press for a few minutes with an iron which has been set to a medium heat. Most fresh grease stains will be liquified by the heat and will then be absorbed by the blotting paper. If necessary, repeat several times, using a clean section of the blotting paper for each operation.

Spatters on Brick

When paint is accidently spattered on unpainted brick, the spots are quite difficult to remove by ordinary means, even when they are fresh. One trick that usually works is to rub over the spatters with another piece of brick. The brick dust created will usually pick up the paint and will camouflage what little remains. A broken piece of concrete will work the same way on spattered cement or stucco.

Carpet Burns

Cigarette burns in carpeting are a frequent problem in many households. To remove them easily (if the burn mark is not deep), rub lightly with fine, dry steel wool. If the burn goes deeper, then the ends of the burnt tufts should be clipped off carefully with a scissors first. Then scrub again with the steel wool till all black marks disappear.

Grease Spots in Rug

To remove grease spots from rugs, try mixing a paste of dry cleaning fluid and powdered starch. Spread over the grease spot, and let dry completely. Then carefully scrape and vacuum up the dry dust. Stubborn spots may require several applications.

Grease on Wood Floors

Grease spilled on wood floors should be quickly cleaned or it will make a lasting stain. Wipe up the surface liquid

with a rag dampened in carbon tetrachloride or a petro-
leum-base solvent. If a stain remains, cover the spot with
an inch-thick layer of sawdust that has been liberally wet
down with a solvent. After a few hours sweep the sawdust
into a dustpan. The stain should be drawn up into the
sawdust.

Grease on Concrete Floor

To remove spilled oil or grease from an unpainted concrete floor, cover the stained area with a one-half-inch-thick
layer of dry, powdered portland cement. Let this stand for
twenty-four hours or more, then sweep it up. Scrub any re-
maining stains with a piece of burlap dipped in a solvent
such as varnolene or mineral spirits. In stubborn cases
apply a second application of cement, saturate with solvent,
and let stand overnight before sweeping up. This method
usually works best during warm weather, or if the floor is
in a room which is partially heated.

Control Dust

To keep down the clouds of dust that are stirred up in
confined areas when dirty floors are being swept, moisten-
ing with water is often resorted to. One way to apply just
the right amount of water without puddling is to spray it
on. Use a garden sprayer or a vacuum cleaner spraying
attachment filled with water.

Sweeping Compound

During the summer months, freshly cut grass clippings
can be used as an excellent sweeping compound when dusty
concrete floors in basement or garage need cleaning. The
green clippings should be sprinkled liberally over the floor
before sweeping. They will effectively hold down the dust
and will make the cleaning job easier and faster.

Scrubbing Floors

When floors must be heavily scrubbed with steel wool
or sponges, your fingers and arms will often tire rapidly
because of the heavy downward pressure required. One
way to help ease this job is to place an ordinary brick over

the steel wool or sponge while scrubbing. Its weight will apply a good deal of the pressure needed, and will enable you to do the job faster and easier.

Wood Counters

Wooden cutting boards or counter tops which have become stained and discolored can be given a new lease on life by first scrubbing thoroughly with scouring powder. Then use household bleach to remove stubborn stains. The natural wood color and finish can be restored by rubbing in several coats of boiled linseed oil, applied twenty-four hours apart. Mop each coat on liberally, then wipe off the excess after about fifteen minutes.

Garage Drippings

To prevent an unsightly, greasy mess on the garage floor where oil drips down from the bottom of the automobile engine, place a long flat metal pan on the spot and leave it there at all times. Keep this pan half full of sand or fine sawdust so as to absorb the drippings, and clean it out whenever the sand or sawdust becomes saturated.

Preserve Garbage Cans

Garbage cans usually rust out along the bottom first. To lengthen their life, and to make them easier to keep clean and sanitary when they are older, the bottoms can be coated with asphalt paint. A cupful of paint can be poured onto the bottom of the can and then rolled around until all seams and crevices are filled. Be sure to scrub clean beforehand, and carry the coating up about ten or twelve inches from the bottom around the sides.

Sink Stains

To remove stubborn rust stains or other discolorations from kitchen sinks and from light-colored bathroom tile and fixtures, try using oxalic acid crystals. Sprinkle some of the crystals over a wet cloth and rub vigorously over the stained areas. Then rinse off. If the stain remains, make a thin paste of the acid crystals and hot water, and let soak over the spot till it dries. Wash off with plenty of hot water and repeat the procedure if necessary.

Tile Stains

When the joints between bathroom tiles become extremely dirty and stained so that no amount of scrubbing seems to get them clean, the problem can often be solved by using either a common laundry bleach or a little ordinary kerosene rather than the usual cleansing agents. Scrub on vigorously with a small, stiff-bristled brush such as an old toothbrush (Fig. 46). Allow bleach (if used) to soak on the surface for several minutes. Rinse thoroughly and repeat if necessary.

Fig. 46

Mildew

To get rid of mildew on upholstered fabrics or luggage, try sponging lightly with a clean cloth which has been dampened with an equal-part mixture of denatured alcohol and water. Allow to dry in fresh air if possible. This will also get rid of the musty odor in most cases.

Wastepaper Baskets

To prevent dust, pencil shavings and other dirt from sticking to the bottom of wastepaper baskets when they are emptied, coat the inside and bottom with a liquid self-polishing wax after cleaning it out. Not only will this keep it from getting so messy, it will also protect metal baskets from rusting.

Protect Fingernails

When the lady or the man of the house does gardening, painting or similar jobs which result in dirty hands, caked dirt often works its way under the fingernails and is very difficult to remove. To prevent this, scratch the fingernails beforehand over the top of a cake of soap. The soap will become embedded under the nails and will prevent dirt from lodging there. The soap can be easily washed out with water after the job is done.

Dusting Corners

To ease the task of brushing dust out from corners of cabinets or woodwork, try trimming an old whisk broom or short-bristled paint brush so that its edge comes to a tapered point. For trimming the bristles use a razor blade or sharp knife.

Grass Stains

Green grass stains are often difficult to remove from many types of clothing. A solvent that usually works well on cotton and on most colorfast materials is ordinary rubbing alcohol. For safety's sake, test first on a corner of the garment. If it tests out all right, rub the alcohol well into the grass stain until it is removed. Then wash in the usual manner.

Plaster Stains

When plaster drops onto painted surfaces during a patching job, the stain can be easily removed by first scraping lightly with steel wool, working carefully so as not to injure the painted surface. Then sponge the area with a little lemon juice diluted with three parts water, and rinse with a damp cloth immediately afterward.

FURNITURE REPAIRS

Blistered Veneer

When veneer on furniture blisters up, a repair can be made by first slitting the blister with a razor blade, cutting parallel to the grain. Cover with a pad of cloth which has been moistened in hot water and let this soak on the surface till the veneer softens. Remove the cloth and immediately work some fresh stainproof glue under the blistered surface with a thin spatula or knife blade. Press flat, cover with waxed paper, and apply weights to hold the veneer in place until the glue has dried. Glue which has oozed out can then be carefully scraped off, and a fresh coat of wax or furniture polish applied to effectively hide the repair.

Hiding Scratches

Scratches on furniture can often be obliterated by wiping with a solution consisting of equal parts of boiled linseed oil, turpentine and white vinegar. Stir the ingredients well, and apply with a soft woolen cloth. Then polish with a dry lintless cloth.

Water Marks

When a beverage glass leaves a white ring on the top of a piece of furniture, the mark can often be removed completely by rubbing lightly with a little chemically pure petroleum. Let this soak overnight, then rub off with a clean cloth in the morning. In most cases the mark will be lightened considerably, or may even have disappeared completely.

Furniture Dents

To remove most dents in wooden furniture, start by first washing off all of the old polish or wax with turpentine or other solvent. Then fill the dent with water, cover with a damp cloth, and lay a warm iron directly over it till the water steams it away. Do not touch the iron directly to the finish (to avoid burning) and set at moderate heat only. In some cases the finish may turn white or show other signs of damage, so if complete refinishing on the surface is not planned, a test should be made in an inconspicuous corner first.

White Scratches

Scratches in dark furniture usually stand out because they look white. They can be quickly touched up with ordinary iodine. Apply with the point of a toothpick or a fine, pointed brush (Fig. 47). Lighten the color if neces-

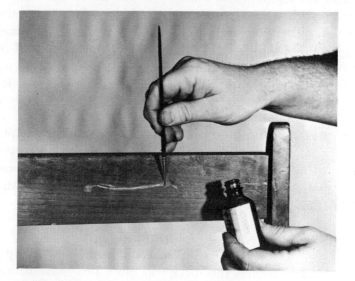

Fig. 47

sary by diluting the solution with small amounts of alcohol. Let dry thoroughly, then cover with a liberal application of furniture polish.

White Spots

When white blemishes or rings occur on furniture because a hot object was placed on the surface, the mark can usually be removed with camphorated oil. Pour a little of the oil onto a soft clean cloth and wipe over the blemish with moderate pressure. Then rub vigorously with a second piece of clean dry cloth, and finish off with a light application of furniture wax or polish.

Marble Protection

Marble table tops and counter tops are highly decorative, but they are also quite susceptible to staining by spilled liquids. To protect the marble, coat periodically with a hard, automobile-type paste wax, then buff to a high shine. In addition, wipe up spilled liquids as quickly as possible.

Burns on Furniture

Slight burns in furniture finishes can often be removed by careful rubbing with powdered pumice stone (available at paint and hardware stores). Use a piece of felt wrapped around a small wooden block to do the rubbing. Dip the felt in water, squeeze almost dry, then sprinkle pumice over the burned area and rub carefully. Try to limit the rubbing to as small an area as possible. On very small burns, better control can be achieved with a piece of felt wrapped around one fingertip. After the burn mark has been rubbed out, rub again with powdered rottenstone to remove scratch marks and restore the polish. Allow to dry overnight, then touch up with a thin coat of shellac after cleaning off all powder. Finish by applying wax or polish after the patch has dried.

Fabric Stains

Stains in fabrics are particularly difficult to remove because of the danger of spreading and absorption. One handy trick to remember is to use clean sheets of white blotting paper to draw out the stain after the appropriate solvent has been applied to dissolve it. For example, apply carbon tetrachloride to lipstick stains or grease stains; turpentine to crayon marks; and warm water to freshly spilled coffee or tea stains. In each case sponge the solvent on with a minimum of rubbing, then press on the blotting paper. If necessary, repeat several times.

Cure for Sticking Drawers

When drawers in cabinets or chests start to stick during humid weather the trouble is most often due to absorption of moisture which has caused the wood to swell. To cure this condition, open the drawer enough to enable you to slide in a forty-watt bulb and socket. Use an extension cord to plug this in, and let the lamp burn for several hours. This will dry the wood out sufficiently to enable the drawer to slide free once more. To prevent recurrence of this condition, give the insides and edges of the drawer a coat of clear shellac or resin sealer. This will seal the raw wood and prevent future moisture absorption.

Fix Carvings

Chipped ornamental moldings on picture frames, furniture, and other woodwork can be easily repaired by re-

Fig. 48

building the missing sections with wood putty (Fig. 48). This is sold in powder form, and when mixed with water dries into a hard, wood-like material which can be carved, sanded or sawed.

Prevent Tarnishing

To keep decorative brass hardware on furniture or cabinets from tarnishing, protect it with a coat of clear lacquer applied by brush or spray bomb. Brush on carefully so as to avoid getting the lacquer on nearby finished surfaces since it may soften up or blister the finish. If a lacquer spray bomb is used, protect the surrounding woodwork by use of masking tape and sheets of newspaper.

Lubricate Drawers

When drawers in chests or desks show signs of sticking, try rubbing the edges with paste wax to lubricate them. Wipe off dust, then apply only a light coating of wax. Buff off the excess to prevent stickiness. This also works well on windows and small sliding cabinet doors.

Furniture Joints

When glued joints on chairs, tables or other furniture start to loosen up, repairs can often be made by re-gluing. To avoid the necessity for completely disassembling the piece, try injecting glue into the joint with the aid of a small eyedropper. Spread the joints apart slightly before doing this, and warm the glue beforehand by immersing the container in hot water for several minutes so that it will flow more easily.

To Lengthen Leg

A quick way to solve the problem of lengthening one short leg on chairs or tables is to use some type of quick-hardening wood putty or plastic filler. Sand off all paint or varnish and drive a small tack into the bottom so that the head projects a fraction of an inch. Then put a blob of the plastic on a piece of aluminum foil and press the leg into it until the chair or table sits level. Allow the plastic to dry, then remove the excess with a fine-toothed saw and sandpaper. Finish off by painting or staining to match.

Warped Doors

Wide doors and cabinet doors which have warped can frequently be straightened out by applying heat with an ordinary heat lamp on the convex side. Do not hold so close that the surface finish is scorched, and remove the source of heat as soon as the warp disappears. Then immediately coat both sides and edges with sealer to prevent re-entry of moisture.

Sectional Furniture

To keep pieces of sectional furniture from sliding apart, ordinary metal hooks and eyes can be screwed into the length cabinets these hooks and eyes can be put into the back where they will not be noticed. On sofas or multiple legs along the back side. The pieces then can be hooked together until the housewife is ready to unhook them when it is necessary to slide them apart for cleaning.

INDEX